Eye-Popping

3-D Bulletin Boards that Teach

Susan L. Lingo

Susan Lingo Books™

www.susanlingobooks.com

*Teach them to your children and
to their children after them.*
—Deuteronomy 4:9

Eye-Popping 3-D Bulletin Boards That Teach
© 2009 Susan L. Lingo

Published by Susan Lingo Books, Loveland, Colorado 80538.

Interior design and cover by Susan L. Lingo

ISBN 978-1-935147-08-4
Printed in the United States of America

contents

What's so cool about *bulletin boards* anyway?

They inspire kids' imaginations!

Inspire imaginations and share the excitement of three-dimensional, interactive displays with these simple-to-create bulletin boards, door displays, appealing ceilings, table toppers, and more. Bulletin boards and other visual displays dramatize your lessons, encourage interaction, and offer kids a chance to participate in classroom planning and preparation. These aren't your run-of-the-mill bulletin boards—these are displays that won't sit still! Interactive bulletin boards invite kids to take an active part in learning and make the most of teachable spaces in your room. Included in each bulletin board or display pattern in this book are suggestions for ways to include your kids in the construction of bulletin boards and enriching "Extension Activities" that encourage cooperative teamwork and community building experiences—all focused around the exciting room display you've created.

They engage kids through serving!

If you're a classroom teacher, you're already the leader-elect of your own "bulletin board ministry." Bulletin board ministry? Well, bulletin boards are a way of serving. And visual displays can teach and tell about Jesus. But who has time to put up catchy displays? Where can you find patterns that aren't the same stale ideas you've already seen? How do you gather people and motivate them to attach paper shapes to a board or wall? The answer lies in creating displays that are as fun to make as they are to learn from! And kids can play an essential role in your bulletin board ministry! How? *By letting kids help plan, prepare, construct, and dismantle visual displays in the room!* Organize your kids into their own fun, exciting ministry called: "Awesome Construction Teams" or "ACTs."

Form groups of three to six kids and let them sign up in advance for each month of the year. Help inspire enthusiasm and creativity by leaving this book next to the sign up sheet for kids to look at when they're choosing a month. Have each ACT choose members to be the Titling Team, the Background Builders, and the Border Guards. The Titling Team is responsible for putting up the letters or titles in the displays. The Background Builders have the job of choosing backgrounds, then putting them in place. And the Border Guards are responsible for choosing and creating colorful borders for the displays. You'll supply the materials and any major pattern pieces. Your special construction teams will supply the elbow grease and inspiration! (See the next page for tips on turning your kid into a nifty bulletin board ministry team!)

They're terrific teaching tools!

The key to effective displays is rooted in uniqueness and "learnability." On & Off the Wall Bulletin Boards is designed to equip you with simple techniques to create dynamite 3-D bulletin boards and other unique displays. The first section of this book offers tips and suggestions for unusual materials and step-by-step "construction instructions" for letters, backgrounds, borders, and 3-D display components that include: risers, platforms, pedestals, ramps, sills, and more. The second section includes inventive ideas for bulletin boards and other visual displays. Each bulletin board or display idea contains suggestions for snappy, kid-centered activities and projects that revolve around your display themes — making them valuable teaching tools!

They will serve you for years!

With the help of *Bulletin Boards That Teach,* creating excitement classroom displays is a snap! Make several new bulletin boards each year and you'll soon have a plethora of dynamite displays to delight your kids year after year — with minimal time and expense. Store finished displays in long, flat boxes or slide them into garbage bags to lay flat. Label each display and attach a simple sketch or photograph to each so you'll have a reminder of the final product the next time you're ready to display it. Organize displays by season, month, or theme, or another filing system. This keeps your bulletin boards at one's fingertips for years to come.

Use your imagination! Try a unique technique! Think "off the wall"! And have fun creating exciting, interactive displays that invite kids to take a second look!

ORGANIZE YOUR KIDS INTO A COOL CONSTRUCTION TEAM!

Organizing a bulletin board ministry geared for kids, not only will take some of the workload from you, but will provide kids with the chance to make a difference in their class! Offering kids opportunities to help plan, prepare, construct, and dismantle bulletin boards and other visual displays pays big dividends in...

* **teamwork**
* **responsibility**
* **service**
* **communication skills**
* **stewardship of materials and time**

Giving kids a bit of responsibility helps them learn about serving others— and God!

An effective bulletin board ministry may even inspire older kids to volunteer their talents for displays outside of their immediate classrooms. And kids love the chance to proudly show their parents and peers what projects they've worked on with friends! Here are a few handy tips and helps to get you started!

1 Make special badges for kids to wear during the construction and dismantling of displays to add an "official" touch. Official membership cards can also add a sense of pride and belonging to this special ministry. Photocopy the patterns for the card and badge (from page 8) on stiff card stock. Invite kids to color the items then cut them out. Laminate the cards and badges or cover them with clear, self-adhesive contact paper for added durability.

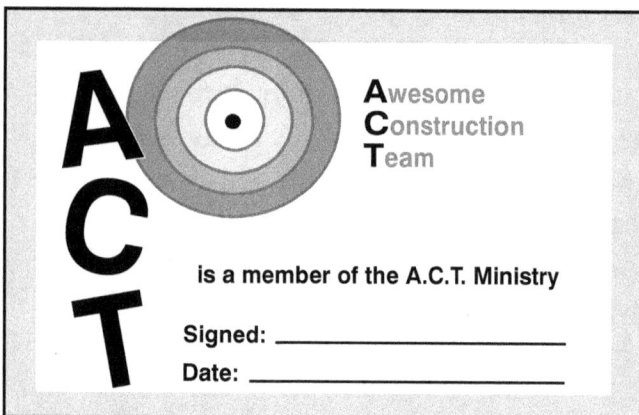

Awesome **C**onstruction **T**eam

is a member of the A.C.T. Ministry

Signed: _____

Date: _____

Awesome Construction Team

2 Collect all of the materials you'll need for the day you plan to construct your bulletin board. This makes set-up time quick and easy! Check out the simple supply list on this page for commonly used materials, papers, and other supplies.

3 Materials used in constructing classroom displays are usually easy to find at most craft stores, office supply stores, and discount centers. Garage sales and church members' attics are also good places to find papers, fabric scraps, or other decorative touches!

SUPPLY CHECKLIST

❏ scissors
❏ stapler & staples
❏ clear tape
❏ push pins
❏ construction paper
❏ markers
❏ crayons
❏ pencils & erasers
❏ measuring tape
❏ a ruler or yardstick
❏ yarn or string
❏ fishing line
❏ precut letters
❏ letter stencils

4 Older kids can usually handle the responsibility of putting up bulletins boards independently, But don't overlook the many ways young children can help, too! Even kindergartners are wonderful construction assistants and enjoy handing you materials to staple or pin as they offer suggestions for pattern placements.

5 On dismantling day, ask your ACT'ers to gently remove the patterns and letters from the displays, and store them in an under-the-bed storage box or in large garbage bags to lay flat. This will keep your displays dry, safe, and usable year after year.

Awesome
Construction
Team

is a member of the A.C.T. Ministry

Signed: _____

Date: _____

Awesome
Construction
Team

is a member of the A.C.T. Ministry

Signed: _____

Date: _____

Awesome
Construction
Team

is a member of the A.C.T. Ministry

Signed: _____

Date: _____

TRICKS OF THE TRADE

BACKGROUNDS & BORDERS

Borders and backgrounds can make or break entire displays, yet they're the most neglected aspect of bulletin boards.

✔

Effective use of borders and backgrounds creates eye-interest and invites interaction between your display and kids.

What's lemonade without the lemons? What's summer without a vacation? And what's a bulletin board without a background or border? Boring! Borders and backgrounds can make or break entire displays, yet they're the most neglected aspect of bulletin boards. Exactly what role do backgrounds and borders play in effective visual displays? Backgrounds and borders...

➤ **add continuity to displays,**

➤ **bring cohesion between titles and elements of your displays,**

➤ **create eye appeal and invite interaction between the display and kids,**

➤ **help elements of displays stand out and be noticed,**

➤ **define the boundaries of displays and corral the central focus,**

➤ **add a neat, finished touch to edges.**

Backgrounds and borders may seem inconsequential and even bothersome—but they're the backbones of effective classroom and hallway displays. Use the following tips and suggestions for creating striking backgrounds and bold borders that invite audiences to take a closer look!

BODACIOUS BACKGROUNDS

Covering the areas behind your display with kaleidoscope colors, perky patterns, or unique materials sets the stage for effective displays. Simply choose a background medium and securely attach it with staples, pins, or rolled duct tape and voilà—an instant invitation to view your display! Traditional backgrounds include construction paper and colored butcher or craft paper which is available at craft and school supply stores in 3½-foot-wide rolls. Simply purchase the amount of background paper you'll need for your particular display area.

Materials that offer loads of coverage for the money include: rolls of wallpaper, gift-wrapping paper, shelf paper, wide rolls of aluminum foil, colorful garbage bags, and paper grocery sacks.

Solid-colored paper backdrops give you the added advantage of leaving them in place through many displays. Consider using blue, black, brown, or yellow paper to avoid numerous background changes throughout the year.

Though solid-colored papers are fine to use, you may be daring and want more zip and pizzazz than solid colors offer. There are many specialty coverings that give striking, novel effects. For displays involving travel or vehicles, use old atlas pages or maps to cover backgrounds. Old phone book pages make great backdrops for displays focusing on communication or spreading God's Word. Specialty gift wraps add sparkling effects and launch even the most basic displays into orbit. Metallic holographic designs add punch to displays that contain a lot of text but few graphics. Glittery star patterns create heavenly effects on your walls or doors and fish-patterned papers make superb "ponds."

Fabric can be used just as effectively as paper for backgrounds. Green hop sack creates sensory "grass," while blue satin makes delightful, shimmery "oceans" and cloudless "skies." Paper, gift wraps, fabrics—the possibilities are endless. Use your imagination to mix and match solid papers, printed gift wraps, and sensory fabrics, and you'll be on the fast track to dynamite displays!

BOLD BORDERS

Border trims establish boundaries for your displays and help focus attention to the centers of bulletin boards. Bright colors, shiny materials, and interesting shapes create border interest. And the best part? Most borders can be made instantly! Precut borders in a wide variety of colors and patterns are available at most school supply stores and through office and school supply

Try some of these nifty backgrounds to make your bulletin boards really zing and pop to life!

- holographic gift wrap
- old maps
- vinyl shower curtain liners
- satin fabric
- tactile felt or hop sack cloth
- soft velveteen
- colored cork tiles

catalogs. The Appendix at the back of this book lists addresses for school supply companies that produce or stock a large variety of precut borders. Keep an eye out for rolls of wide ribbon on sale at craft and discount stores. Ribbons come in wonderful patterns, electric colors, and a myriad of textures—and ribbons can be easily pinned, stapled, or taped to displays in a snap. Inexpensive, instant, and reusable, ribbon trims are invaluable for borders.

Other unusual border materials you may wish to use include:

➤ **men's neckties**

➤ **individually wrapped candies**

➤ **scarves and bandannas**

➤ **belts and wide sashes**

➤ **artificial vines and flowers**

➤ **old greeting cards**

➤ **crepe paper**

➤ **balloons**

Kids love coming up with ideas for unique borders— then bringing in the items to complete their plans!

Two unique, yet simple, border treatments are the wave and the picture frame. To create the wave, all you need are a stapler and colorful construction paper. Measure the perimeter of your display area, and multiply by two. Then cut 3-inch-wide strips of construction paper to equal the total. Attach one end of a paper strip at a corner of your display, create roller coaster waves, and glue or tape them into place. Now tape the other end of the strip to the display. Overlap the next paper strip to begin a new series of waves. Continue placing paper strips waves end-to-end around the entire display.

Wave borders give a neat 3-D look to your displays.

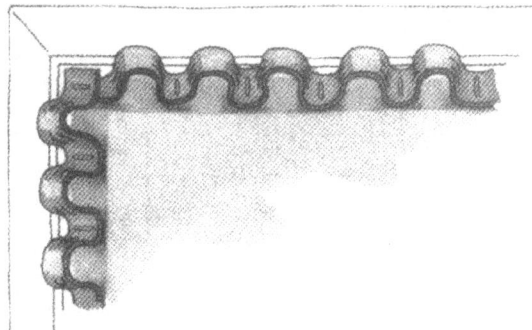

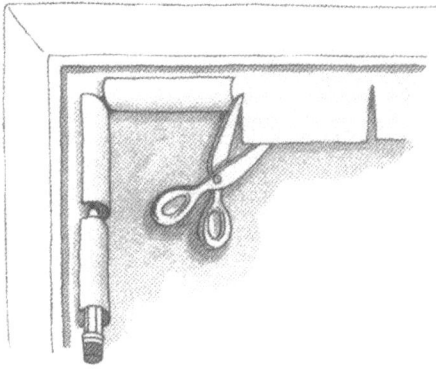

The picture frame border is a simple, yet striking, border kids love to create! All you need for this slick trick are scissors, a pencil, construction paper, and tape or a stapler. Cut enough 4-inch-wide construction paper strips to go around the edges of your display area. Staple or tape the strips to the display, end to end, along the outside edge. Then carefully make 2-inch snips along the border strips. Make a snip every 5-inches around the entire border. Now roll each section around a pencil. Be sure to roll the paper outward, away from the center of the display. The paper will curl outward creating a 3-D picture frame effect around your entire display. Simple, effective — and loads of fun for your ACT'ers!

Remember the fun of cutting out paper dolls? Use the same idea to create custom borders for your displays. Photocopy and use the patterns on the following pages to make your own unique borders. Simply accordion-fold a sheet of paper, then copy or trace a pattern onto the paper. Cut out the pattern, then attach the strips of fun shapes around the edges your display.

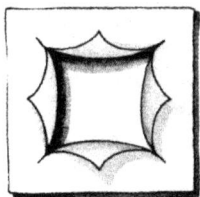

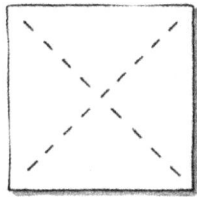

Cut out rows of shapes in an instant using the simple paper doll technique!

Use the picture frame concept to frame kids' artwork. For each frame, simply cut an X in the center of a sheet of construction paper, then curl the sections outward around a pencil. Tape the artwork behind the opening for instant eye-interest!

TRY THIS!

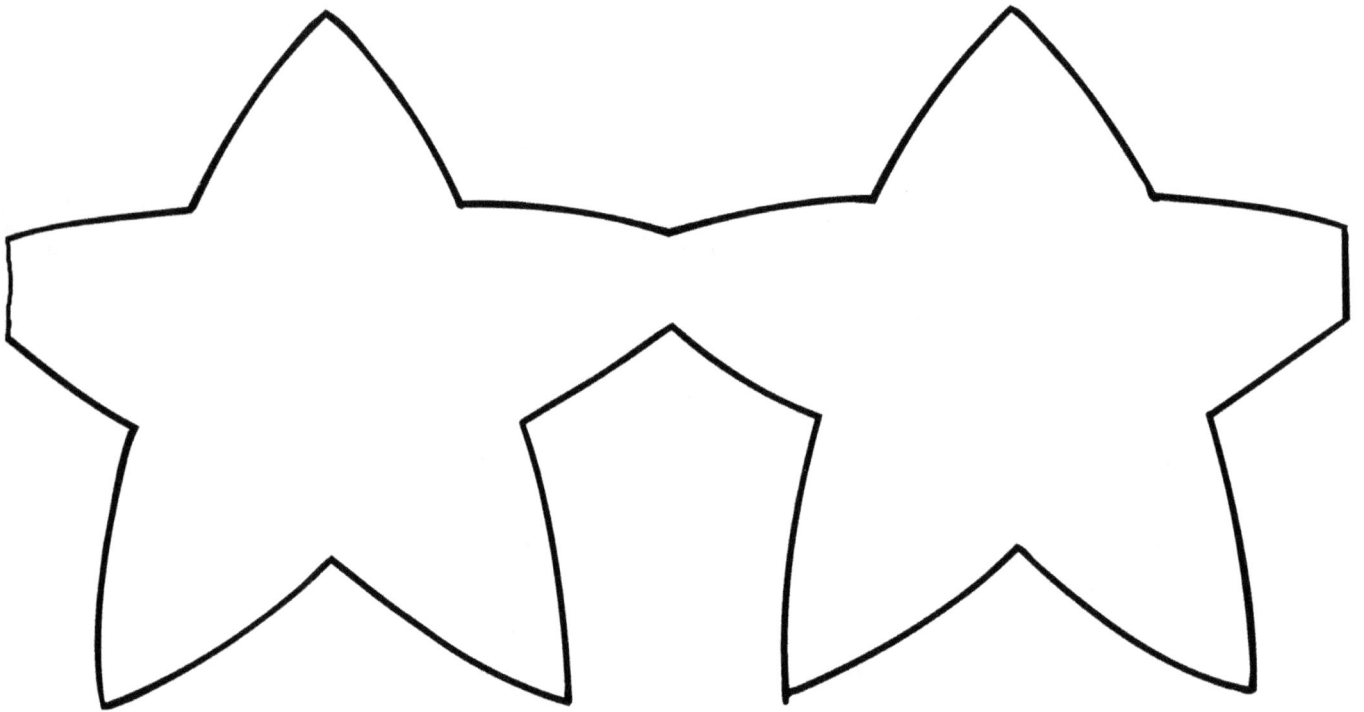

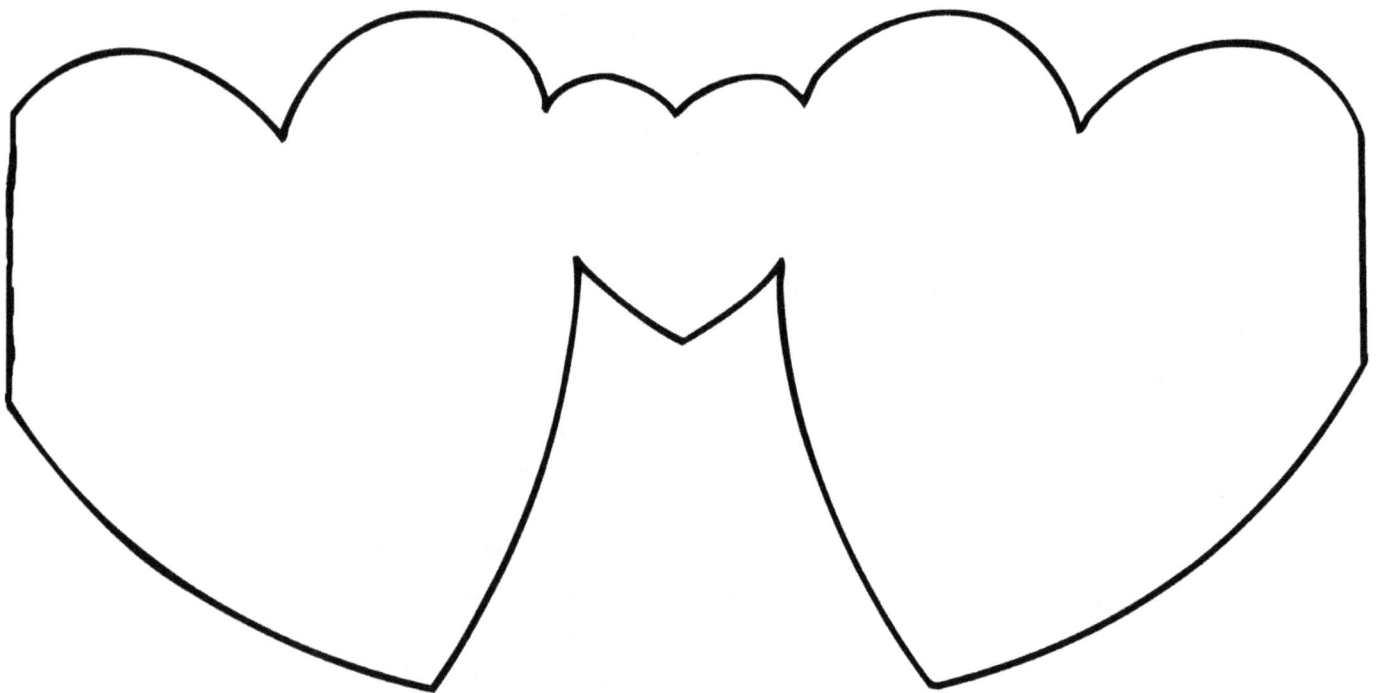

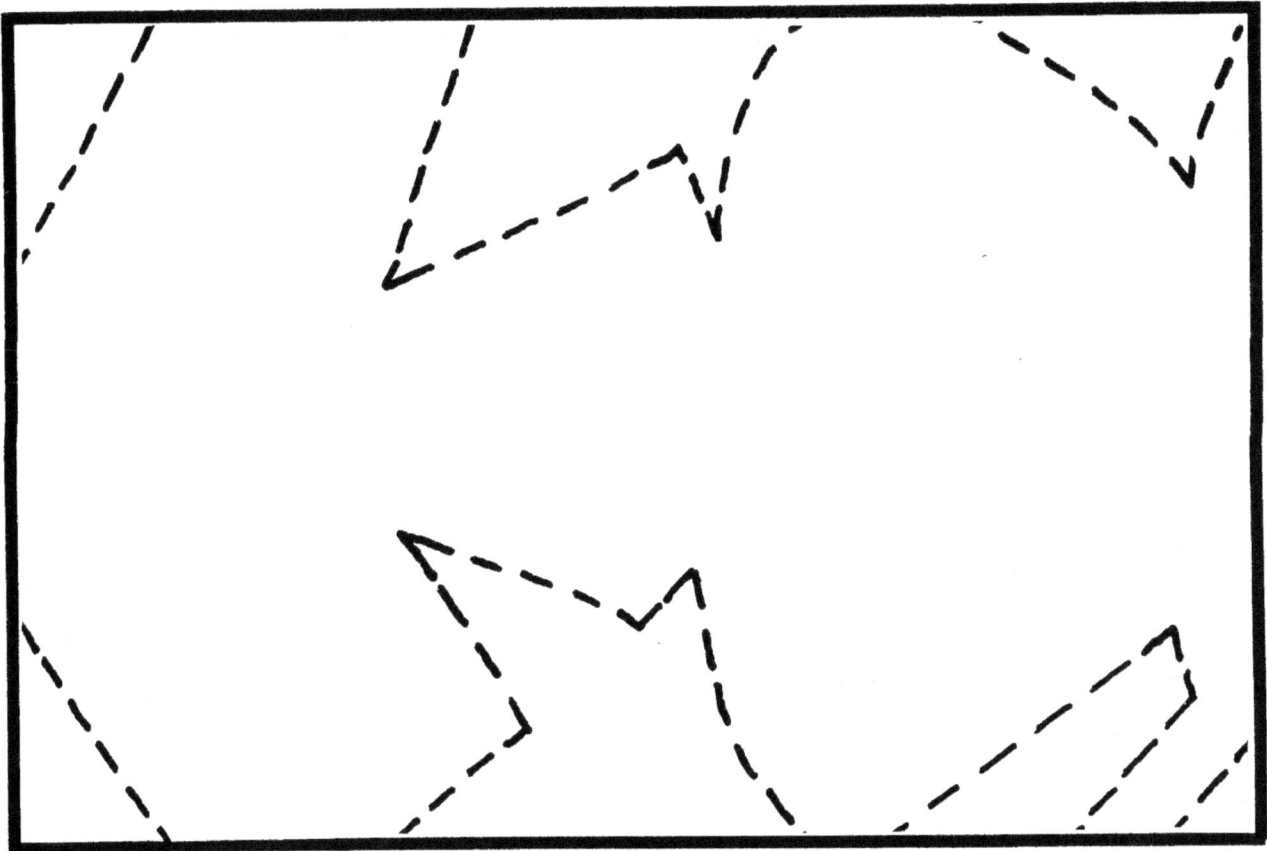

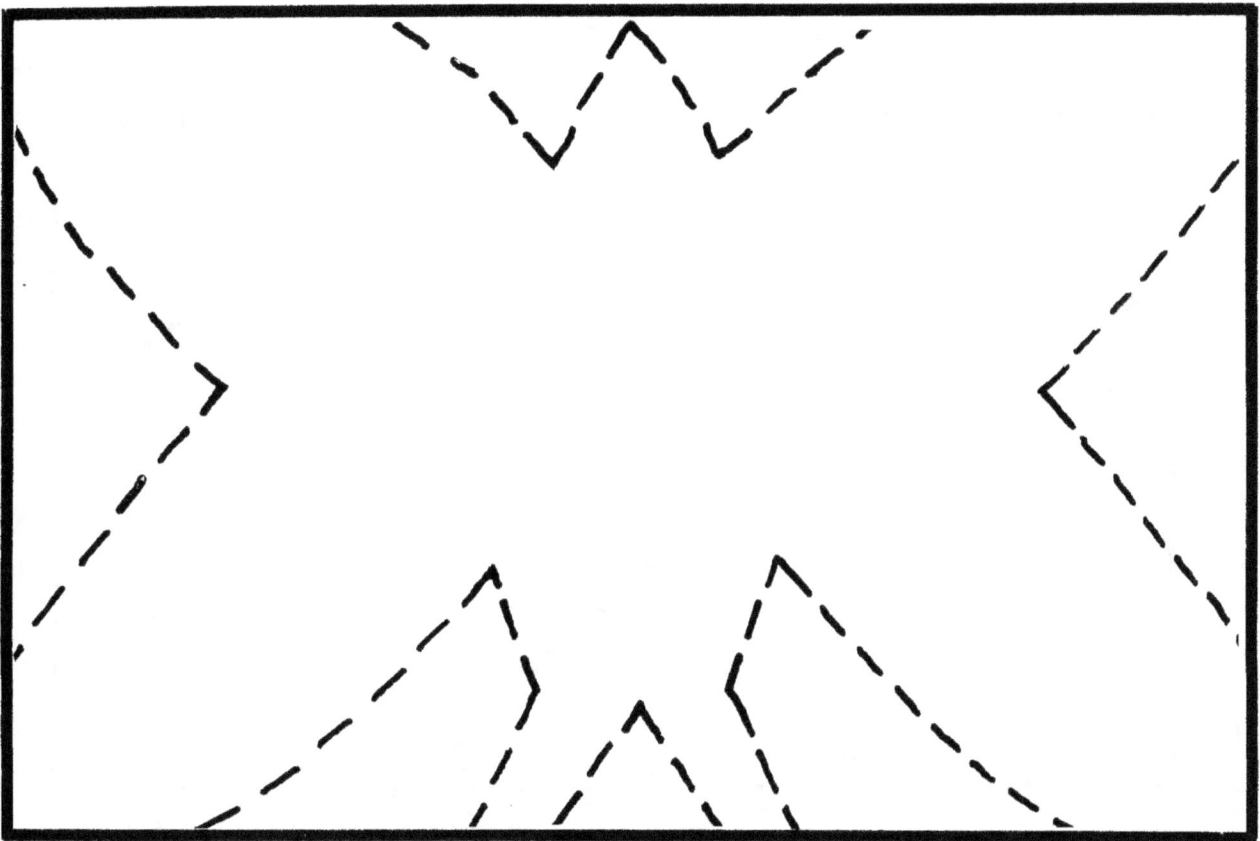

15

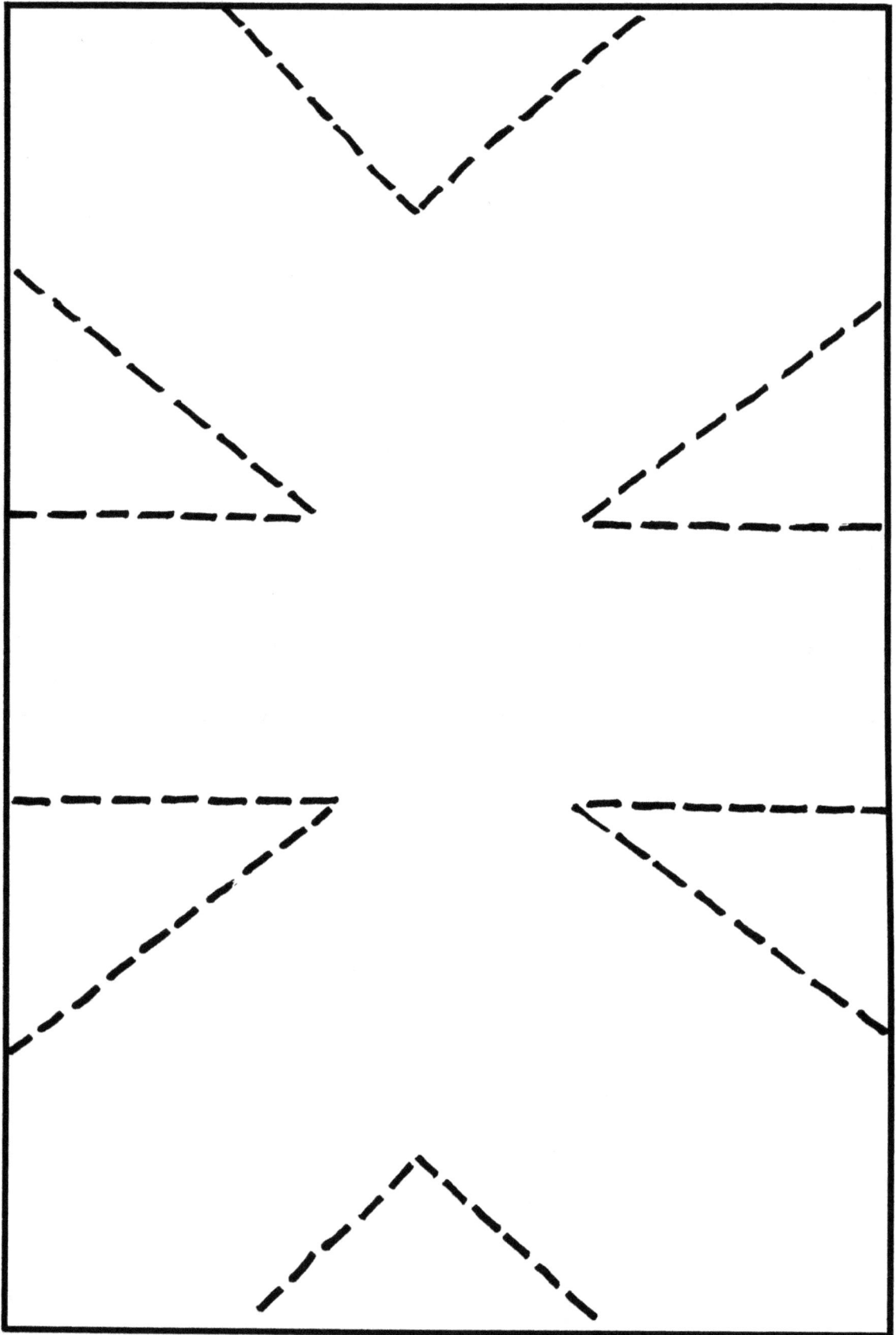

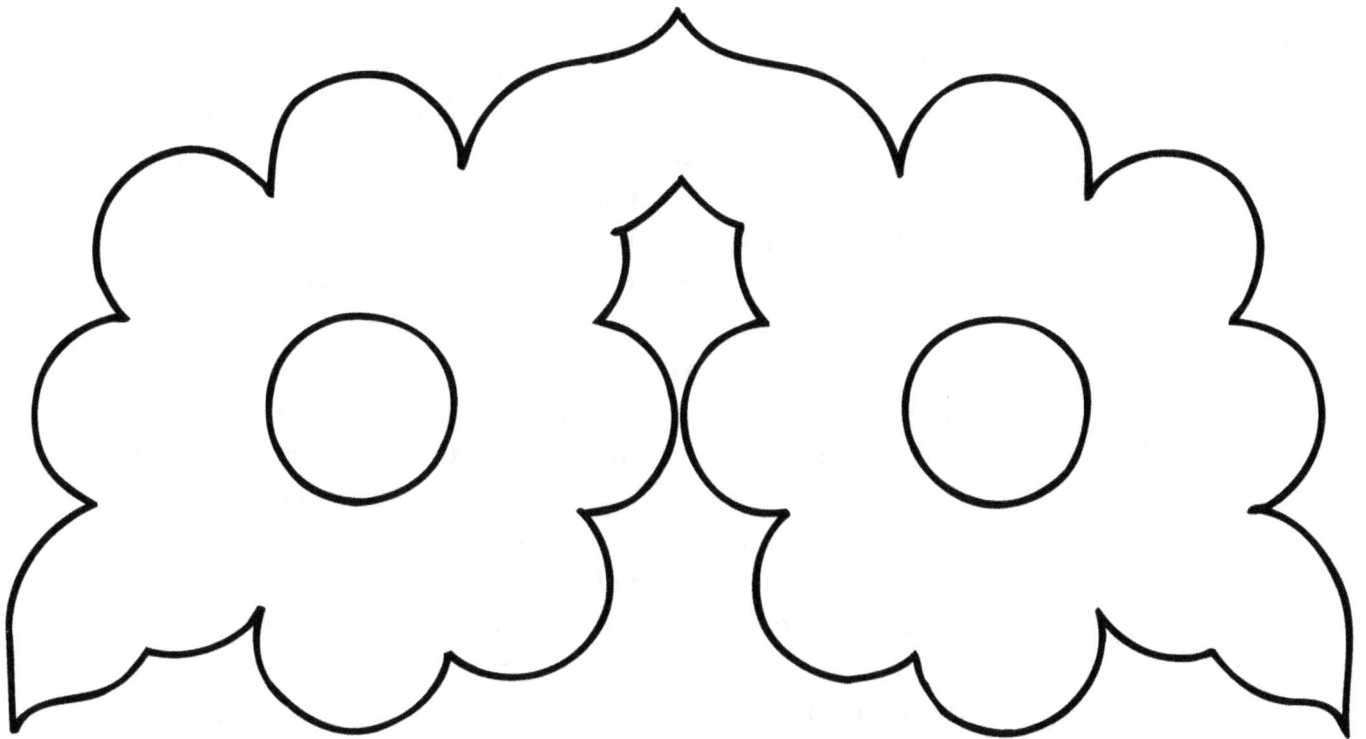

LIVELY LETTERS

What bulletin board chore is more tedious than cutting out letters for titles and display text? Tracing, clipping, snipping, guiding scissors in and out of endless minuscule spaces — it's enough to try the patience of a statue! Take heart because, although letters on most bulletin boards are a must, there are ways to make "lettering" less frustrating, more exciting, and infinitely more effective for your displays. Marvelous materials, title boards, and ingenious storage systems make lettering a snap — you just need to learn the "ABCs" of lettering!

MARVELOUS MATERIALS

Let's begin by crumpling up and tossing out the stale idea that all bulletin board letters are made of construction paper. Sure construction paper works, but so do zillions of other more creative and imaginative materials. Consider using wild, wacky wallpaper letters. Wallpaper is bright and sturdy and can add a variety of amazing sheens and textures to displays. Ask wallpaper stores or decorating centers for free, outdated sample books, then go wild creating extraordinary letters for your displays.

When it comes to letters, think TEXTURE. Sandpaper, grass cloth, corrugated cardboard, aluminum foil, rolled cork, and felt all have great eye appeal and beg to be touched. Remember that the goal of a dynamic display is to bring it off the wall and into the hands and hearts of your kids. Textured letters add an exciting 3-D touch and give new life to old displays.

Create a colorful kaleidoscope of words on bulletin boards. Neon paper "blasts" the words off your display and is available at most print and photocopy centers for nominal costs. Electric blue, shocking pink, vibrant yellow, and outrageous orange give you a lot of "glow for the dough"!

Want a terrific tip for letters in a snap? Simply laminate alphabet-patterned fabric, then cut out the letters! Laminated fabric

---

Think out-of-the-box and off-the-wall when it comes to materials for letters! Try using one of these for more texture, vibrancy, and eye-interest:

- corrugated cardboard
- wallpaper
- laminated fabric
- old greeting cards
- colorful craft foam or felt

letters are bright and fade resistant — and there's no tracing letter patterns or stencils. Laminating cotton fabric is perfectly safe for both fabric and laminating machines, provided there are no staples or pins in the fabric. Another quick tip for cutting out letters: Simply snip loosely around the letters and don't worry about following the outlines exactly — no one will notice your shortcut, especially when you're using laminated fabrics.

There are countless other materials you can use to create exciting letters for your displays. Ribbon, gift wrap, paper grocery sacks, and self-adhesive paper all make great letters, but they do require the use of patterns. At the end of this chapter are a few letter patterns to get you started. Simply reduce or enlarge the selected patterns to fit your needs — or try mixing and matching various letter fonts to stylize the words on your displays and create really eye-catching effects.

3-D LETTERING AND TITLE BOARDS

Once you've created letters for your bulletin board or display, they may either be attached one-by-one or placed on a title board. If you're constructing a title letter-by-letter, consider using a dramatic technique to lift the words off the display surface. *Pedestals* and *risers* attached behind each letter (or the first letter in each word) create shadows beneath the letters and give the words a dramatic 3-D look. Directions for making and attaching pedestals and risers will be explained in Chapter 3.

Pedestals and risers give your letters a 3-D look.

Title boards are quick to create and kid-friendly for your ACT'ers. Simply use bright markers, paint, paint pens, or glitter glue to write your title text across a wide strip of poster board, foam board, rolled cork, or cardboard. Use a pencil to lightly mark guidelines on the title board for each word before actually writing. Many a

> Lift letters off of bulletin boards or door displays by attaching them to 3-D pedestals or risers. Creating shadows invites displays to leap off the wall!

title board has fallen victim to "squished, downhill" words and writing!

After your title board is lettered, glue ribbon or fabric braid around the edges to create a finished look. Then simply attach the board directly to your display by using rolled duct tape or by placing your title board on pedestals, a sill, or a shelf. (See Chapter 3 for directions on constructing pedestals, sills, and shelves.) Well-made title boards will last for years of use and enjoyment.

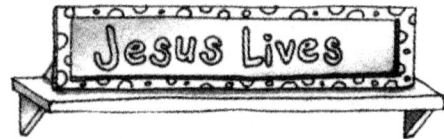

LETTER STORAGE SYSTEMS

Once you've taken the time to create a collection of striking letters or titles, it's important to store them for safekeeping so they may be used year after year. Some people prefer to make multiples of one or two letter fonts, while others enjoy creating a unique title or text for each bulletin board or display. If you choose to create custom titles and texts, keep them in self-locking plastic bags with your display elements, then store the entire displays in under-the-bed storage boxes or large plastic garbage bags that will lay flat for storage. It's a good idea to keep a sketch or photo with each display, showing how the display was arranged and what words were used.

If you're creating multiple letters of one or two fonts, you may wish to consider using the following rule of thumb for the number of letters to prepare:

➤ **Letters A, E, I, O, U: ten of each letter**

➤ **Letters D, S, L, N, R, N, T: ten of each letter**

➤ **Remaining letters: at least four of each letter**

> **Keep letters, shapes, backgrounds, and other elements of your displays safe by storing them in plastic tubs, under-the-bed boxes, or even garbage bags. Consider hanging them from hangers with clips on either end and covering them with clear plastic dry-cleaning bags.**

Store prepared letters in large manila envelopes by letter style, or use handy accordion folders for vowels, common consonants, other letters, numbers, and symbols. By keeping letters and displays organized, they'll be ready to put up at a moment's notice, and you'll save hours of work!

If you have spare time in class, provide patterns, pencils, paper, and scissors and invite kids to help trace and cut out letters to use in your displays.

TERRIFIC TIPS

Use pins, staples, or rolled tape to attach letters to your displays.

Cut out multiple letters by stacking four sheets of paper in a pile. Trace the letter pattern on the top sheet, then cut through the layers simultaneously.

Be sure letters are in proportion to your display: too small and titles are lost; too large and titles are overpowering.

Consider purchasing ready-made letters from school supply stores. (See Appendix.)

Create unusual letters from torn paper. Or cut letters with pinking shears to jazz up the edges of plain letters shapes.

LETTER PATTERNS

A B C

D E F

H I J K

L M N

LETTER PATTERNS

O P Q

R S T

U V W

X Y Z

LETTER PATTERNS

A B C

D E F

H I J K

L M N

LETTER PATTERNS

O P Q

R S T

U V W

X Y Z

A B C
D E F
H I J K
L M N

O P Q
R S T
U V W
X Y Z

SPECIAL EFFECTS

If you're taking the time to create an eye-popping display, go the extra mile with special effects that are as simple to make as they are dramatic. Sills, awnings, arches, pedestals, ramps, pull-wires, peek-overs, and shelves produce sensational results with minimum preparation and are easy enough for kids to make. Choose and use any of the following special effects, and your displays will dazzle with real pizzazz and panache.

PEDESTALS

Pedestals add a dramatic touch to the elements of any display. In essence, pedestals are low bases attached to the backs of display figures and letters. They literally lift figures off flat surfaces, creating shadows which produce 3-D effects. Constructed from stiff paper, poster board, or cardboard, pedestals are reusable for display after display. Pedestals are especially effective for letters, central display figures, and displaying kids' framed artwork on bulletin boards.

How to construct pedestals:

Step 1: For every two or three pedestals, you'll need a cardboard tube. Empty bathroom tissue or paper towel tubes work especially well for pedestals. Decide how high you desire each pedestal to be, then cut the tubes accordingly.

Step 2: Make snips of equal length around the ends of each tube about one-fourth to one-half inch apart. Then spread the ends outward to create a flared effect.

Step 3: Tape or glue

> **Hidden pedestals made from stiff foam board or poster board give an exceptional look to kids' artwork, display letters, and more!**

each figure or letter to one end of the pedestal, then attach the other end of the pedestal to your display with tape, pins, or staples.

SILLS AND SHELVES

Ever wonder what to do with all those empty shoe boxes and lids your closet seems to accumulate? Put them to use on your bulletin boards! Snappy shelves and striking display sills allow you to:

> ➤ **suspend display figures,**
> ➤ **show off title boards and other figures,**
> ➤ **hang kids' artwork in a clever way, and**
> ➤ **create depth on an otherwise flat surface.**

Made from shoe box lids, colored paper, and tape, sills and shelves will last for years of repeated use on bulletin boards and other displays.

How to construct sills and shelves:

Step 1: Cover the outside of box lids or shallow boxes with colorful paper. Consider using patterned self-adhesive paper for it's durability and "stick-to-itiveness."

Step 2: Use thumbtacks or rolled duct tape to attach the sills and shelves to flat surfaces. Sills are one box lid in length, while shelves may be created by attaching two or more sills end to end across the top of your display area.

Step 3: Tape letters to the edges of shelves, suspend figures with fishing line from sills or shelves, or set title boards on the tops of shelves.

Shelves made from colorful cardboard, poster board, or foam board create an exciting dimension to displays. Wrap ribbon, fabric, or festive gift wrap around the front and side edges of shelves for even more eye appeal!

RAMPS

Ramps are used to secure title boards and other figures to sills and shelves. They're a snap to make from poster board and give stability to a myriad of display elements, including title letters and boards.

How to construct ramps:

Step 1: Cut a 3-by-9-inch strip of poster board for each ramp. You may need to adjust the size if your title board is very large. You'll need at least two ramps for each title board.

Step 2: Fold the paper strip into thirds, then tape the ends and push the strip into a triangular shape.

Step 3: Tape the figure or one end of the title board to the perpendicular side of the ramp. Then tape the bottom of the ramp to the sill or shelf.

PULL-WIRES

What's more exciting and inviting than action wires that actually move items on a bulletin board? Kids love pulling action wires and watching fish leap from papery waves, stars fluttering up and down from the ceiling, and boats actually sailing across make-believe oceans. When pull-wires are attached to doors, bulletin boards come alive each time someone enters the room! And action pull-wires are great to use in classroom games—use them for ending relay races or to pull question and answer cards from a "mystery question box" on the bulletin board.

Each pull-wire is easily made from fishing line and three small eyelet screws available at hardware stores. (Since eyelets actually screw into a display surface, use them only for bulletin boards or wooden doors that can withstand a few small holes.) Pull-wires are a snap to make and loads of fun for kids (and adults!) to manipulate.

How to construct pull-wires:

Step 1: Decide what elements on your display will have pull-wires attached, then "map out" courses for the wires to travel. You must include two or three points of pull for each wire: one where your figure is hanging, one where you wish the wire to

> Otherwise flat title boards will jump off the wall, door, or other display when used with small cardboard, poster board, or foam board ramps.

be pulled, and for big displays, one point of pull along the top. **Step 2:** Screw the eyelets directly into the bulletin board or door at your chosen points of pull.

Step 3: Thread fishing line through each set of eyelets and add a few extra inches or feet of fishing line, depending on how easy it will be for your kids to reach. Cut the fishing line at the desired length.

Step 4: Tie a paper clip or metal washer to the end of the line nearest the place the wire will be pulled. Thread the fishing line through the path of pull, then tape a figure on the other end of the fishing line. Now pull the paper clip or washer to be sure your figure moves up and down.

eyelet screw

Kids enjoy the whimsy and interactive appeal of pull-wires that enable static bulletin board figures to suddenly move!

AWNINGS

Awnings on bulletin boards and other displays give a cozy look and focus attention on what lies beneath. Expansion awnings span the entire tops of bulletin boards, while partial awnings accent particular areas of a display. Awnings are made from foam board or shallow box lids and have papery scalloped edges to give an airy look. Again, well-made awnings will last many years.

How to construct expansion awnings:

Step 1: Cut a piece of foam board in half. Place the halves end to end and duct tape them together to create a long, narrow rectangle. If your display is longer than this length, don't use an awning as it may sag and collapse.

Step 2: Cut a 3-inch-wide scallop from colorful paper and tape it along three edges of the awning.

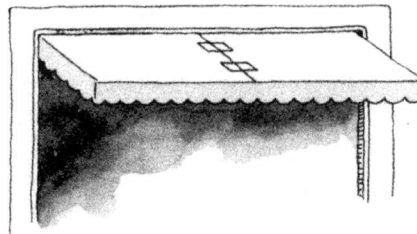

Bulletin Boards That Teach

Step 3: Use long hatpins, or duct tape to attach the awning to the top of your display.

How to construct partial awnings:

Step 1: Prepare a shallow box lid as per the directions for sills and shelves.

Step 2: Cut a 2-inch-wide scallop from colorful paper and tape it along three edges of the awning.

Step 3: Use thumb-tacks, pins, or duct tape to attach the awning to one area of your display.

PEEK-OVERS

Peek-a-boo—I see you! Peek-overs are great special effects for bulletin boards, window tops, and the tops of doorways. Whimsical, colorful, and uniquely clever, peek-overs add fun to any classroom decor—and kids love making peek-overs as much as peeking at them!

How to construct peek-overs:

Step 1: Draw or trace a peek-over pattern. Cut out and trace the pattern on colorful poster board.

Step 2: Cut out the peek-over pieces, then embellish them with markers, glitter glue, sequins, fabric, or ribbon. You may wish to laminate the pieces for extra durability and fade resistance.

Step 3: Position the peek-overs above your bulletin board, window, or doorway so that they look down over your classroom. Use rolled duct tape to secure the peek-overs in place.

Don't overlook the effective use of peek-over figures to embellish doorways and windows in your classroom!

ARCHES

Arches add a playful touch to bulletin boards. Soft, pliable lines create interest and eye appeal and turn otherwise plain displays into 3-D show stoppers. Use arches to cleverly hold rows of letters or figures.

How to construct arches:

Step 1: Place your letters or figures in a row on the floor, then measure the length of their span. Cut a 2-inch-wide poster board strip that length. You may need to tape two strips of poster board together.

Step 2: Make a fold 3 inches long at each end of the poster board strip. Staple, pin, or duct tape the folded ends to your display surface.

If your arch to too long, it may sag in the center. Either use a narrow pedestal as a center support or choose another technique to display your items.

Step 3: Tape the letters or figures across the arch. Be sure the figures are evenly spaced.

Equipped with as many snazzy special effects as any movie studio, you're ready to produce the most exciting, inviting, and motivating displays you or your kids have ever imagined. Be innovative! Go wild! And have fabulous fun bringing your bulletin board ministry to new life!

✔ Hula hoops cut in half and attached to a display using duct tape make nifty awnings when a lightweight fabric or gift wrapping paper are added.

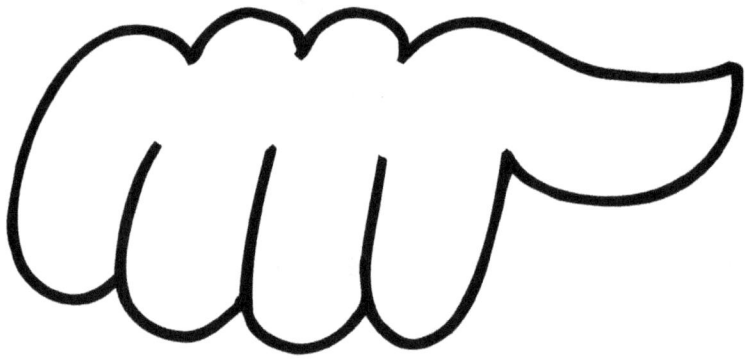

DYNAMITE DISPLAYS

SIMPLE SUPPLIES

- scissors
- tape and stapler
- gift wrap or yellow background paper
- yellow crepe paper
- black and yellow construction paper
- white poster board
- curling ribbon
- party hats
- party horns

SIMPLE DIRECTIONS

1 Cover the bulletin board with brightly colored or patterned gift wrap or yellow background paper. Add a border of twisted crepe paper.

2 Construct and attach four small sills to the top portion of your display. Use black construction paper to cut out one set of letters to spell the word "Year," then cut out two sets of letters to spell the word "New."

3 Cut the letters to spell the word "Life" from yellow construction paper. Attach ramps to the letters, then attach the letters to form the phrases "New Year" and "New Life" on top of the sills.

4 Make a calendar from a sheet of white poster board. Instead of a month's name, title the calendar, **"Forever."** Be sure to add the days of the week and number the squares up to 31.

5 Attach the calendar to the center of the display.

6 Attach party hats, curling ribbon, and party horns between the phrases "New Year" and "New Life." Add curling ribbon to the corners of the calendar.

More Learning Fun!

➤ Photocopy or purchase a small calendar of the new year (or new school year) for each child. Let kids use markers or crayons to color the calendars. As kids work, talk about the new year and how many people consider the new year a time to make a fresh start in their lives. Point out that, when we love Jesus, we don't have to wait for a new year to begin anew—every day is new with Jesus! Encourage kids to make a fresh start by serving Jesus in ways such as helping others, being kind to kids who need a friend, and learning more about Jesus.

➤ Set out a variety of tasty ingredients such as crackers, peanut butter, marshmallow creme, raisins, chocolate chips, and dried apple bits. Hand children plastic knives and invite them to create "new" tasty treats. As kids are enjoying their goodies, point out that people can make new recipes but that only Jesus can make lives new. Then share a prayer thanking Jesus for our new lives in Him.

SIMPLE SUPPLIES

➤ scissors
➤ tape and stapler
➤ blue, white, black, and orange construction paper
➤ silver glitter glue
➤ black and white tempera paints
➤ 6 square boxes
➤ duct tape
➤ paper lunch sacks
➤ newspapers
➤ batting

SIMPLE DIRECTIONS

1 Cut 11-inch blue construction paper letters to make the title, *"Be COOL … Flock to Jesus!"* Tape the letters across one area of the wall.

2 Cut four white construction paper icicles. Outline the icicles with silver glitter glue. Tape an icicle to the bottom of each letter of the word "cool."

3 Use white tempera paint to paint the six boxes. After they're completely dry, create an igloo by stacking the boxes against the wall or using duct tape to attach them to the wall.

4 Make a flock of perky penguins by first stuffing paper lunch sacks full of newspaper. Paint the sacks with black tempera paint, leaving an area blank for a white chest. Once the black paint has dried, paint the blank area on each sack with white tempera paint.

5 Cut black construction paper wings and tape or glue them to the sides of the penguins.

6 Cut orange construction paper beaks and webbed feet. Tape the beaks and feet in place. Use white construction paper to create tiny eyes for the penguins. Attach your flock of penguins to the wall using duct tape.

7 Use duct tape to attach batting "snow drifts" to the wall around the igloo and flock of penguins.

TERRIFIC TIP!

Make colored glitter glue by mixing glitter, white craft glue, and a bit of powdered tempera paint.

More Learning Fun!

➤ Have children create their own penguins and tape them to the wall. You may wish to have each child write his or her name on the penguin's chest. Tell children that flocks of sheep and birds and even penguins have leaders to follow—and that our special leader is Jesus!

➤ Let younger children pretend to be waddling penguins as they sing the following song (to the song to the tune of "London Bridge").

Little penguins, march around—
Flap your wings, touch the ground.
Little penguins shout, "Yahoo!"
Jesus—loves—you!

SIMPLE DIRECTIONS

SIMPLE SUPPLIES

- scissors
- tape and stapler
- gift wrap or fabric with heart pattern
- red, white, pink construction paper
- red poster board
- white poster board
- pictures of children (magazine photos or photos from your class)
- pattern for Jesus from page 87

1 Cover the bulletin board with heart-print gift wrap or fabric or pink background paper. Cut out a red, white, and pink construction paper border, using the heart border pattern on page 14.

2 Cut title letters from white construction paper. You may wish to use pink or red construction paper to spell the word "love."

3 Cut a large number 1 from construction paper. Tape a pedestal on the back of the number to "lift" it off the bulletin board. Attach the other title letters flush to the display.

4 Cut a large heart from red poster board. Make sure the heart is at least 3-feet wide. Staple the bottom and sides of the heart to the bulletin board, leaving it loose enough so that you can stuff it with crumpled newspaper. Staple the top edge of the heart when it's "puffy" and looks 3-D.

5 Create a 3-inch-wide poster board arch to span the heart shape. Attach the arch so it bows outward across the center of the heart.

5 Photocopy, enlarge, and color the Jesus figure from page 87. Choose photos of children from magazines or use real photos of the kids in your class! Mount the photos on stiff paper.

6 Tape the figure of Jesus to the center of the arch. Tape figures of the children on either side of Jesus, spacing them out so that they span the entire arch.

TERRIFIC TIP!

Let kids make paper doll figures of themselves! Color the figures and write kids' names on them, then attach them to your special display for a truly personal touch!

More Learning Fun!

➤ Let children point to the figures of the children on the bulletin board and tell you where they think each child might be from, such as Mexico, Africa, or China. Explain that God loves everyone in the world and wants us to love them, too.

➤ Cut a construction paper heart in as many pieces as there are children in the room. Provide tape and give kids a few minutes to reconstruct the heart on a wall. When they're finished with the puzzle, read aloud John 13:34; 15:12, 17; and 1 John 4:16-19. Talk about how we want a heart that's complete in Jesus—Jesus' love for us is perfect, and we're to love others as Jesus loves us.

➤ Invite kids to make "I-Love-You" cards from poster board or card stock paper. Embellish the cards by using stickers, ribbon, lace, sequins, and markers. Have children present their "cards of love" to the special people in their lives.

SIMPLE SUPPLIES

➤ scissors

➤ tape or stapler

➤ cloud-patterned gift wrap or blue background paper

➤ brown foam board

➤ 2 sheets of sturdy white poster board

➤ string or yarn

➤ construction paper or gift wrap (for the kites)

➤ patterns from page 83

SIMPLE DIRECTIONS

1 Cover the bulletin board with cloud-patterned gift wrap or light blue butcher or background paper. This busy display won't require a border or special title.

2 Cut brown foam board into 4 X 6-inch pieces to use as bricks. Arrange the bricks in the center of the display to represent a wall.

3 Construct a 3-inch-wide poster board arch to travel around the base of the wall.

4 Photocopy, enlarge, and color patterns for Joshua (you'll need one figure), seven priests, and four soldiers (page 83). Color and cut out the patterns (set the horns and shields aside for the next step). Attach the figures as shown in the illustration. When you're finished, it should look like a grand processional around the wall with Joshua leading the way!

5 Cut 12 large kites from festive gift wrap or colorful construction paper. Tape or glue horn cutouts to seven of the kites and shield cutouts to four of the kites. Draw a large cross on the last kite. Tape string or twine to the kites and let the ends dangle. (Be sure the lengths of string or yarn are long enough to reach the characters on the bulletin board.)

6 Let kids pin the ends of the kites strings to the appropriate figures on the display. The priests will be flying kites with horns, the soldiers will be holding kites with shields, and Joshua's kite will be the one with the cross to show that he followed the Lord in amazing ways

TERRIFIC TIP!

• Try using stone or brick-patterned wall paper for Jericho's wall.

• Let kids color stones or bricks using crayons or tempera paints to use as paper weights. Glue felt dots to the bottoms of the bricks.

More Learning Fun!

➤ Read the story of Joshua at Jericho. Have kids hold up seven fingers each time they hear the word "seven" during the story. Explain that the number seven is often referred to as "God's number." Then play a game of the age-old classic—Seven Up. Choose seven (or fewer) kids to stand in front of the room. Have the rest of the kids cover their eyes and hold their thumbs up. The children standing may each silently choose a child by putting down a thumb and returning to the front of the room. Then have the other children guess who pushed their thumbs down.

➤ Make a classroom kite using large, plastic garbage bags, clear packing tape, and two yardsticks or 3-foot dowel rods. Cut open a plastic garbage bag so it lays flat on the floor. Make a crossbow using clear packing tape and yardsticks or dowel rods, and attach it on the back of the kite. Let kids tape colorful construction paper patterns to the front of the kite. Attach a ball of string to the crossbow. If it's a windy day, launch the kite outside. If wind and space are at a premium, display your colossal kite on a wall inside the church for everyone to admire. Title your display, "Flyin' High for Jesus!"

The Lion and the Lamb

JESUS

Hosea 5:14 | Rev. 5:5 | Hosea 11:10 | John 1:29,36 | I Peter 1:18-19 | Rev. 5:12

SIMPLE SUPPLIES

- scissors
- tape or stapler
- blue background paper
- construction paper
- orange yarn
- batting
- crafts sticks
- fishing line or string
- index cards
- glitter glue

SIMPLE DIRECTIONS

1 Cover the bulletin board with blue butcher paper. Add a green construction paper wavy border.

2 Draw a large simple lion shape and lamb shape on poster board (brown for the lion and white for the lamb). Embellish the lion with an orange felt mane and tail and the sheep with batting fleece or cotton balls. Use a black marker to add ears, noses, mouths, and eyes. Attach the figures to either side of the display.

3 Construct and mount a shelf traversing the top of the display. Create three title boards as shown in the illustration. Mount the title boards on the shelf.

4 Cut out 8-inch-high red construction paper letters to spell the name "Jesus." Hang the letter "J" from the center of the shelf, then tape each successive letter in a downward row as shown in the illustration.

5 Create snowflakes by taping three craft sticks together in a spread-out fashion. Outline each craft stick with glitter glue. Use fishing line to hang the snowflakes from the shelf above the lion. Cut out blue construction paper raindrops and suspend them above the lamb using fishing line.

6 On index cards, write the following Scripture references. For the lion, write: *Hosea 5:14; Hosea 11:10; and Revelation 5:5.* For the lamb, write: *John 1:29, 36; 1 Peter 1:18-19; and Revelation 5:12.* Attach the cards to the appropriate sides of the display.

TERRIFIC TIP!

For a different look, use black background paper behind the lion and bright green behind the sheep to indicate winter to spring!

More Learning Fun!

➤ Let kids make their own lions and lambs to remind them of the different names for Jesus. Hand each child a photocopy of an animal pattern, then let them use felt, batting, and markers to embellish their projects. Have older kids write appropriate Scripture references inside their lions or lambs.

➤ Compare and contrast the ways Jesus is like a lion and a lamb. Then use the Bible to look up other descriptions of Jesus including the rock (Isaiah 26:4), the bread of life (John 6:35), the light (John 8:12), and the way (John 14:6).

Check out the Lion and Lamb Table Topper on the next page!

LION & LAMB
TABLE TOPPER

Hosea 5:14
Hosea 11:10
Revelation 5:5

John 1:29, 36
I Peter 1:18-19
Revelation 5:12

SIMPLE SUPPLIES

➤ scissors & tape
➤ markers
➤ large balloons
➤ drinking straws
➤ florist's foam
➤ construction paper
➤ batting
➤ orange felt or craft foam
➤ curling ribbon
➤ fine-tipped permanent marker
➤ copies of the lion and lamb patterns from pages 94 and 95

SIMPLE DIRECTIONS

1 Inflate and tie two large balloons. Use a permanent marker to write on the balloons the Scripture references for the lion and lamb (see illustration).

2 Tape the balloons to the drinking straws, then poke the ends of the straws into the foam block.

3 Photocopy the lion and lamb patterns (on pages 94 and 95) using brown construction paper for the lion and white construction paper for the lamb. Embellish the animals with orange craft foam or felt (lions' manes) and batting (lambs' fleece). Use markers or crayons to add facial features and ears.

4 Fold the animals as directed. Set the on the table or tape them to the foam block below the balloons on the sides with the appropriate Scripture references.

5 Cut 12-inch-lengths of curling ribbon and curl the pieces. Lay the curled ribbon on top of the foam block between the lion and lamb.

6 Add curled-ribbon streamers to the drinking straws and the top of the foam block.

TERRIFIC TIP!

Write Hosea 5:5 on the lion pattern and Revelation 5:12 on the lamb. Copy the shapes for each child to color, cut out, and fold as a crafty springtime project!

More Learning Fun!

➤ Let children decorate a "Spring Fling" table with colored paper, party plates, and napkins. Place the table topper in the center of the table. Have kids decorate sugar cookies, then invite parents or another class to a spring fling. Let kids read the Scripture references aloud from the Bible. Then say a prayer thanking God for Jesus.

➤ You may wish to use this table topper as a craft idea for older kids. Invite children to create their own table toppers to take home and share with their families.

➤ Invite kids to make several table toppers to donate to a senior citizen's home, children's hospital, or homeless shelter. Include short, springtime notes expressing your care and Christ's love!

SIMPLE SUPPLIES

➤ scissors
➤ tape or stapler
➤ blue background paper
➤ 3-inch-wide rainbow ribbon or crepe paper
➤ silver glitter glue
➤ construction paper
➤ batting or cotton balls
➤ fishing line

SIMPLE DIRECTIONS

1 Cover the bulletin board with blue butcher paper. Add a border using rainbow-striped ribbon or crepe paper.

2 Place a shelf across the top of the bulletin board. Cut out letters 6 inches tall to spell the title, **"God's Promises."** Embellish the letters with glitter glue. Then attach a riser to each letter, and tape the letters to the top of the shelf.

3 Cut out five or six white construction paper clouds. Glue batting on a few clouds, then tape the sensory clouds along the edge of the shelf. Pin or tape the remaining clouds to the bulletin board.

4 Cut out a white construction paper raindrop for each child. Let kids draw small pictures of themselves on their raindrops then outline the edges of the raindrops with glitter glue.

5 Cut varying lengths of fishing line and hand a piece to each child. Have kids tape one end of the fishing line to their raindrops then attach the other ends of the fishing line to the underside of the title shelf.

TERRIFIC TIP

For a sparkling, rainy effect, tape strands of tinsel behind the clouds so it appears to be raining.

More Learning Fun!

➤ Give kids a chance to be affirmed and feel special. Decorate a wooden fruit crate or box, and invite each child to stand on the "podium." Have other kids name ways that person is special, such as "You have a great smile," "You make others feel happy," or "I like how you try hard." Then lead everyone in a rousing "Hip, hip, hooray" for that person. Be sure everyone has a chance to be affirmed.

➤ Use this display in lessons about Noah and the ark. Encourage kids to brainstorm ways that God cared for Noah and the ark inhabitants and ways that God cares for us every day. Point out that God has promised to always care for us.

Jesus Is Alive!

SIMPLE SUPPLIES

➤ tape & scissors
➤ light blue background paper
➤ green calico fabric
➤ wide purple ribbon
➤ purple and white construction paper
➤ batting
➤ paper lunch sack
➤ eyelet screws
➤ patterns of Jesus, angels, disciples (pages 85, 87, 88 or from an old coloring book)

SIMPLE DIRECTIONS

1 Cover the bulletin board with light blue butcher paper. Add a ground line with green calico fabric. Make a border with 3-inch-wide purple ribbon.

2 Cut several large cloud shapes from white construction paper. Glue batting to a few of the clouds, and set the sensory clouds aside. Attach the remaining clouds to the sky.

3 Construct and attach a shelf across the top of the display. Attach the sensory clouds to the front edge of the shelf.

4 Make a title board with the title, "Jesus Is Alive!" Cut the letters from purple construction paper, and add pedestals to the first letters in each word. Attach the title board to the shelf using ramps.

5 Photocopy, enlarge, and color the patterns of Jesus, the disciples, and the angel on pages 85, 87, and 88. Photocopy the patterns onto stiff paper. Cut out the patterns, and attach the figure of the disciples to the lower right side of the bulletin board.

6 Pin or staple an open lunch sack to the lower left side of the display as a "tomb." Attach a ramp to the angel figure and tape it on top of the tomb.

7 Run a pull-wire under the shelf and across the top of the display. Be sure the pull-wire comes down "through" the clouds in the center of the bulletin board. Tape the figure of Jesus on the end of the pull-wire that hangs in the center of the display. You'll want to position the figure so that it appears as if Jesus is talking with the disciples, then rises to heaven when the action wire is pulled.

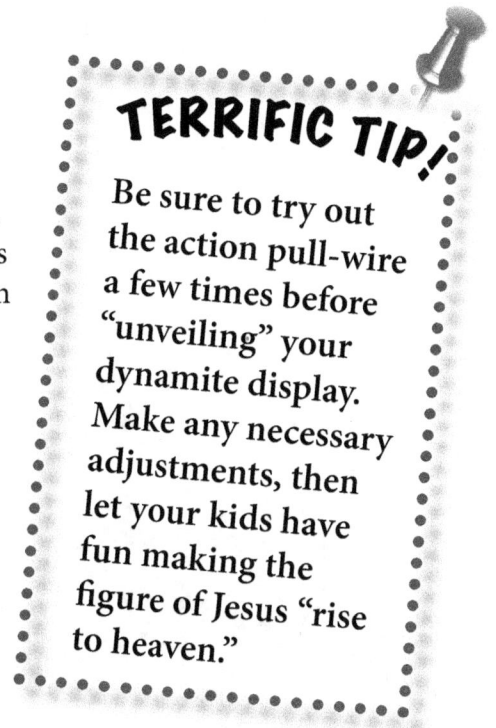

TERRIFIC TIP!

Be sure to try out the action pull-wire a few times before "unveiling" your dynamite display. Make any necessary adjustments, then let your kids have fun making the figure of Jesus "rise to heaven."

More Learning Fun!

➤ Make pop-up ascension cards to celebrate the fact that Jesus is alive. On stiff paper, photocopy the pop-up card pattern on page 90. Let kids use markers, bits of construction paper, and ribbon to decorate their cards. Encourage kids to present their cards to people who might not know the wonderful truth that Jesus is alive.

➤ Whip up a heavenly taste-treat! Let kids pour milk, a few drops of blue food coloring, and instant vanilla pudding in a plastic jar with a tight fitting lid. Give each child a chance to shake the jar for a few seconds, then pour the sky blue pudding into clear, plastic cups. Add a dollop of whipped cream to each cup as a fluffy cloud. As kids enjoy eating their treats, retell the story of Jesus rising up to heaven, and remind kids that Jesus is preparing a place in heaven for us, too.

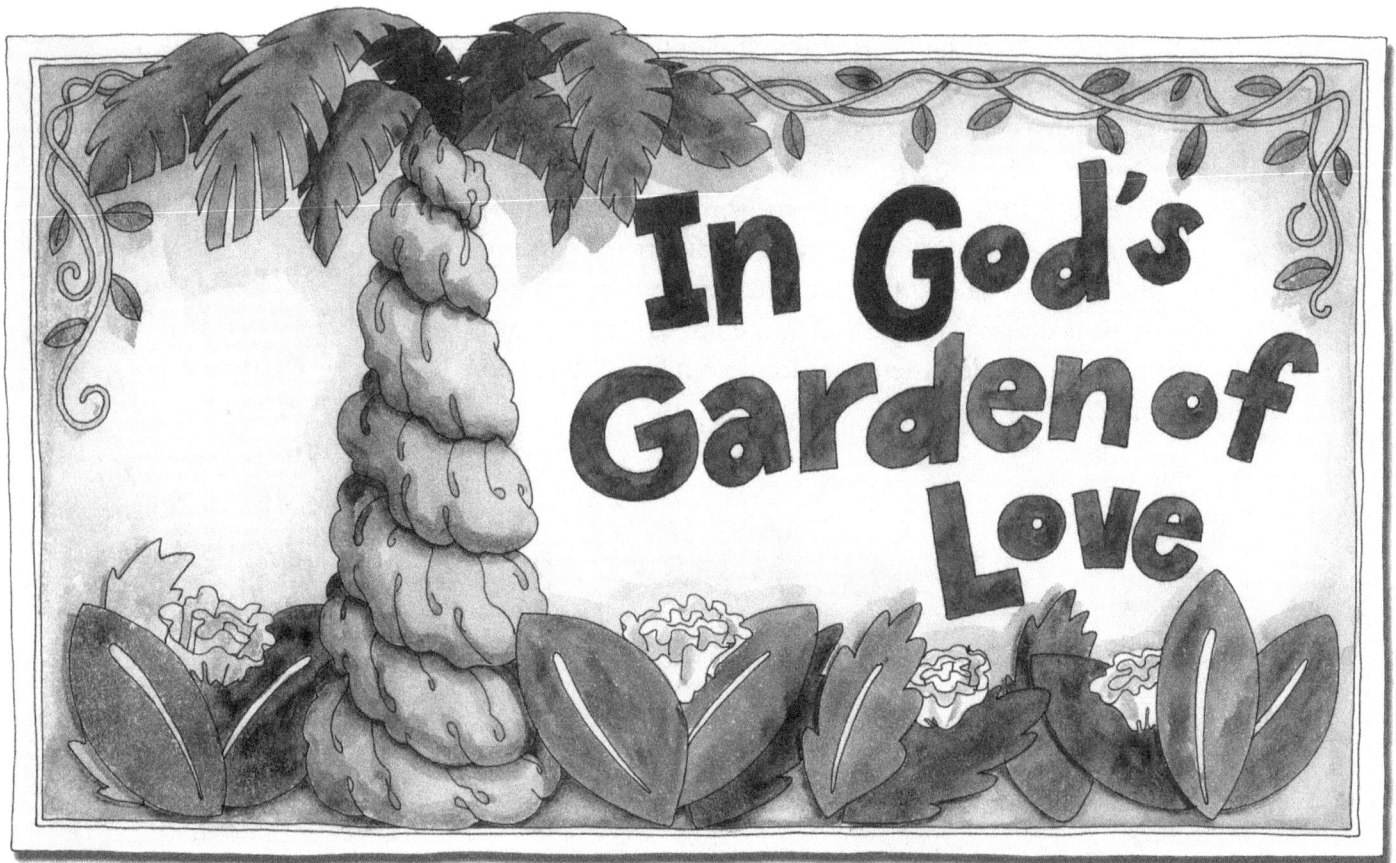

SIMPLE DIRECTIONS

Follow the directions below for creating a wondrous wall display, an appealing ceiling, and a dynamic door.

Wondrous Wall Display

1 Make palm trees by twisting brown paper grocery sacks then taping them to the wall for tree trunks. Cut large palm fronds from green butcher paper or construction paper. Tape the palm fronds to the top of the tree trunks. Be sure to allow some of the fronds to drape away from the wall to create a papery canopy overhead.

2 Use large, cardboard mailing tubes for palm trees in the center of the room. Tape the tubes to the floor with clear packing tape. Add green construction paper fronds.

3 Loop twine around each of the palm trees on the wall for vines.

4 Cut out large, leafy plants from green construction paper, then tape them against the wall. Crumple sheets of bright tissue paper for tropical blossoms, and tape them to the plants.

SIMPLE SUPPLIES

➤ scissors
➤ tape or stapler
➤ brown paper grocery sacks
➤ green background paper
➤ large, cardboard mailing tubes
➤ clear packing tape
➤ construction paper
➤ twine
➤ jungle-print gift wrap

Appealing Ceiling

1 Hang twine across the ceiling for vines. Tear green construction paper leaves and tape them to the twine for a jungle-like effect. You may also wish to tear large paper fronds to hang from the ceiling.

2 Cut tropical birds from jungle-print gift wrap and tape them to the vines and treetops near the ceiling.

3 Add a few bright tissue paper or construction paper flowers among the vines trailing from the ceiling.

Dynamic Door

1 Cover your door with green butcher paper. Tape leafy fronds to a length of twine then loop it around the door. Add a sprinkling of bright paper flowers at the base.

2 Cut jungle animals and birds from the jungle-print gift wrap and tape them on the door and around the walls in the room.

More Learning Fun!

➤ Use the garden display when your class is learning about God's care and provision, the Feast of Tabernacles, the parable of the sower and the seeds, Creation, or the Garden of Eden. Talk about how God's love for us continues to bloom forever, and as we grow in him, we plant seeds of love in others.

➤ Have kids hide heart-shaped "blossoms" around the room and in the display. Form pairs, then go on a "heart safari" and count all the paper hearts each pair sees. Point out that God's love surrounds us every day.

Fishing for You!

SIMPLE SUPPLIES

- tape & scissors
- cloud-print gift wrap
- dark blue, brown, and white construction paper
- shirt box lid
- wood-grained self-adhesive paper
- small basket
- dowel rods or real fishing poles (without hooks!)
- eyelet screws
- fishing line
- sturdy gift warp

SIMPLE DIRECTIONS

1 Cover the bulletin board with cloud-print gift wrap or light blue butcher paper. Add a wave border using dark blue construction paper.

2 Construct and attach a shelf to go across the top of the display. Cut out blue and white letters to make the title, "Fishing for You!" Tape the letters along the front edge of the shelf.

3 Make a wide wave from blue calico fabric, and attach the wave flush across the bottom portion of the bulletin board. Then make a dark blue construction paper wave to also go across the bottom portion of the bulletin board. Be sure the paper wave is narrower than the fabric wave. Attach pedestals to the paper wave, then position and attach the wave to the display.

4 Cover a large shirt box lid with brown, wood-grained self-adhesive paper. Attach the box to the lower right side of the bulletin board for a 3-D fishing dock. Add brown construction paper pilings to the dock.

5 Attach a small wicker or plastic basket to the fishing dock.

6 Rig three or four pull-wires to the display and tie one end of each pull-wire to a real fishing pole or dowel rod. Let the other ends of the pull-wires dangle between the waves. Tie paper clips on the ends of the wires in the waves. Lay the fishing poles on the dock.

7 Cut fish shapes from sturdy gift wrap, laminated fabric, or construction paper. Write each child's name on a fish, then attach the fish to a paper clip. Place the rest of the fish in the basket on the dock.

TERRIFIC TIP!

You may wish to use the fish pattern at the back of the book as a craft project with your display. Let kids color their own fish or make an ocean mobile!

More Learning Fun!

➤ Invite kids to sponge paint fantasy fish. Cut sponges into fish shapes, and let kids use a variety of tempera paints to make colorful fish swimming in the sea. Paint the pictures on long pieces of white shelf paper or sheets of newsprint taped together.

➤ Have kids take turns "landing" the fish. Pull in a fish from the bulletin board and read the name on the fish. That child may tell one way he or she can serve Jesus this week, such as telling a friend about Jesus' love or reading the Bible each night. Be sure each child's name is on a fish for this activity.

➤ Let preschoolers and young children "fish" for balloons. Cut 2-foot-lengths of crepe paper, and put a piece of masking tape on the end of each crepe paper streamer. Blow up and tie off a balloon for each child. Toss the balloons around the room, then let children "cast" their streamers toward balloon "fish" and "reel" in the fish when they stick to the streamers. Leave the streamers attached to the fish and let children pretend their fish are swimming in the sea as they pull the fish around the room.

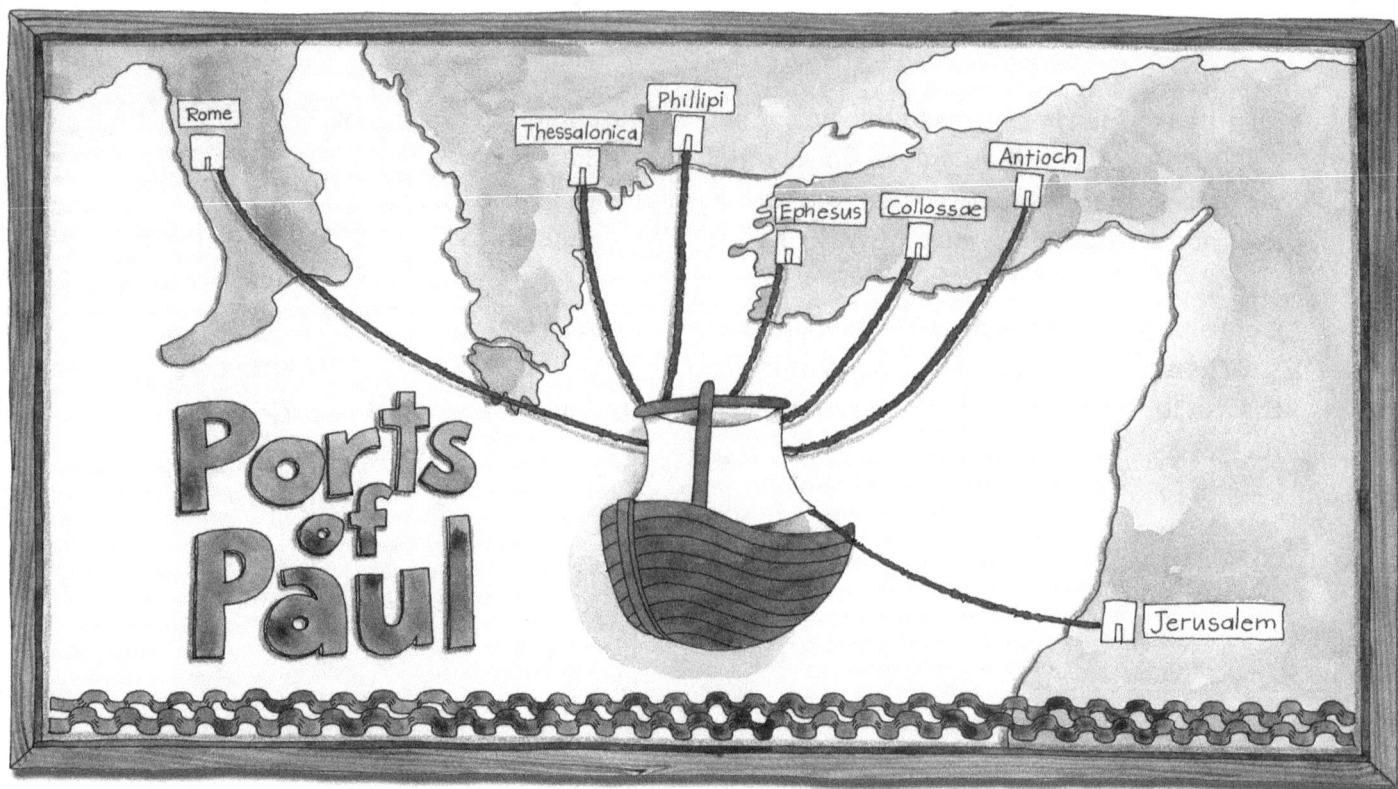

Ports of Paul

Rome · Thessalonica · Phillipi · Ephesus · Collossae · Antioch · Jerusalem

SIMPLE SUPPLIES

➤ scissors
➤ tape & stapler
➤ light blue background paper
➤ brown paper grocery sacks or rolled cork
➤ construction paper
➤ blue, red, yellow, and green yarn
➤ straight pins
➤ markers
➤ pattern for the boat on page 86

SIMPLE DIRECTIONS

1 Cover the bulletin board with light blue butcher paper. Add a shoreline using brown paper grocery sacks, rolled cork, or green wallpaper. For a special touch, sponge paint white caps on the blue water!

2 Cut light and dark blue construction paper into 2-by-10-inch strips. Staple the paper strips in 3-D waves along the bottom of the display.

3 Photocopy, enlarge, and color the boat pattern on page 86 onto stiff paper. Tape the pattern to a pedestal, then attach the boat to the center of the bulletin board. You may wish to add a fabric or paper towel sail for a realistic effect.

4 Cut out nine white construction paper squares for churches. Write one each of the following names on each church: Jerusalem, Antioch, Ephesus, Philippi, Rome, Corinth, and Thessalonica. Position the churches according to the illustration above.

5 Cut 3-foot lengths of each color of yarn. Pin one end of each piece of yarn to the boat. Children will pin the other ends to the churches in the first activity below.

6 Attach blue construction paper letters for the title.

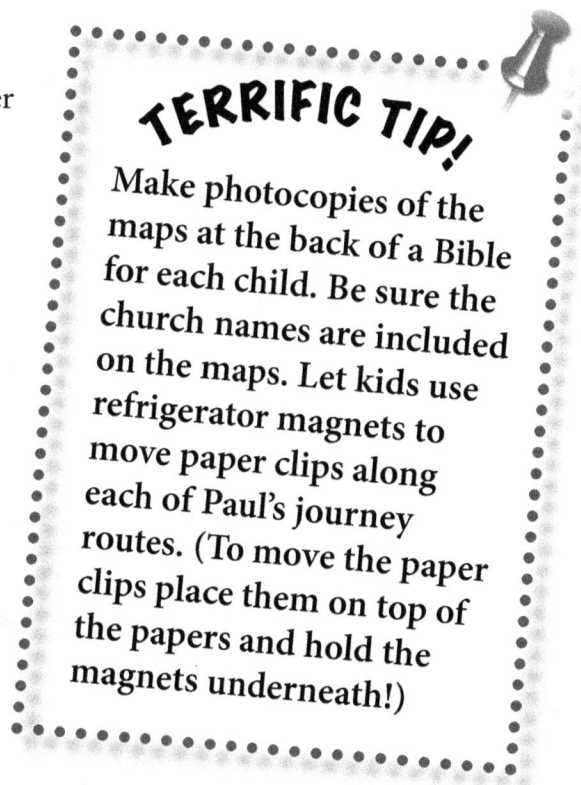

TERRIFIC TIP!

Make photocopies of the maps at the back of a Bible for each child. Be sure the church names are included on the maps. Let kids use refrigerator magnets to move paper clips along each of Paul's journey routes. (To move the paper clips place them on top of the papers and hold the magnets underneath!)

More Learning Fun!

➤ Let kids pin yarn at some of the cities Paul visited during his four journeys to establish new churches. Use blue for the first trip (Antioch), red for the second trip (Jerusalem, Antioch, Thessalonica, Philippi, Corinth, and Ephesus), yellow for his third trip (Antioch, Philippi, Thessalonica, Ephesus, and Corinth), and green for his fourth (Rome). Some churches will have more than one color of yarn attached.

➤ Challenge kids to use their Bibles to find which books in the New Testament were named for churches Paul visited.

Stand on the ROCK of Jesus

SIMPLE SUPPLIES

➤ tape & scissors
➤ cloud-print gift wrap
➤ yellow construction paper
➤ brown butcher paper
➤ newspaper
➤ white poster board
➤ pair of panty hose
➤ pair of socks
➤ tennis shoes
➤ batting
➤ glitter glue
➤ duct tape
➤ markers

SIMPLE DIRECTIONS

1 Cover the bulletin board with cloud-patterned gift wrap or blue background paper. Add a wave border of yellow construction paper.

2 Make a large rock shape from brown butcher paper or brown paper grocery sacks. The rock should be large enough to cover the length of the display and stand about a third of the way to the top. Staple the rock around the bottom and sides, then stuff crumpled newspaper inside to make the rock 3-D. Staple the top edge closed when you finish stuffing the rock with newspaper.

3 Construct and attach a shelf across the top of the display. Make a title board with poster board and markers. Use ramps to attach the title board to the shelf.

4 Stuff the panty hose legs with pillow stuffing. Attach the legs under the shelf so that they hang just above the center of the rock. Slide socks and shoes on the "feet" and position the shoes on top of the rock. You may need to use a bit of duct tape on the edges of the shoes to hold them in place on the rock.

5 Cut a yellow construction paper cross and outline it with glitter glue. Tape the cross on the front of the rock.

More Learning Fun!

➤ Collect large stones for the children to paint or go on a hike and let children collect their own. Paint the rocks with tempera or acrylic paints. As children work, talk about why the word "rock" is a good word to describe Jesus—and why a rock is better to stand on than sand or soil. Tell kids to use their rocks as paperweights to remind them that *Jesus* is the solid rock on which we stand.

➤ You may wish to have children make outlines of their shoes (or use the sneaker pattern at the back of the book) on construction paper. Cut out the shoe shapes, embellish them with markers and glitter glue, then tape them to the rock on the display. Be sure kids put their names on the paper shoes to show *they* are standing firmly on the rock of Jesus!

➤ Teach kids an action rap to remind them to plant their feet on the rock of Jesus. Repeat the following words and actions—then make up a few new "foot frolics" of your own!

Step left, step right—

but STAND on the rock of *(clap)* **Jesus!**

Hop forward, hop back—

but STAND on the rock of *(clap)* **Jesus!**

Heel and toe, tip-tip-toe—

but STAND on the rock of *(clap, clap)* **Jesus!**

HOLD YOUR BANNER HIGH

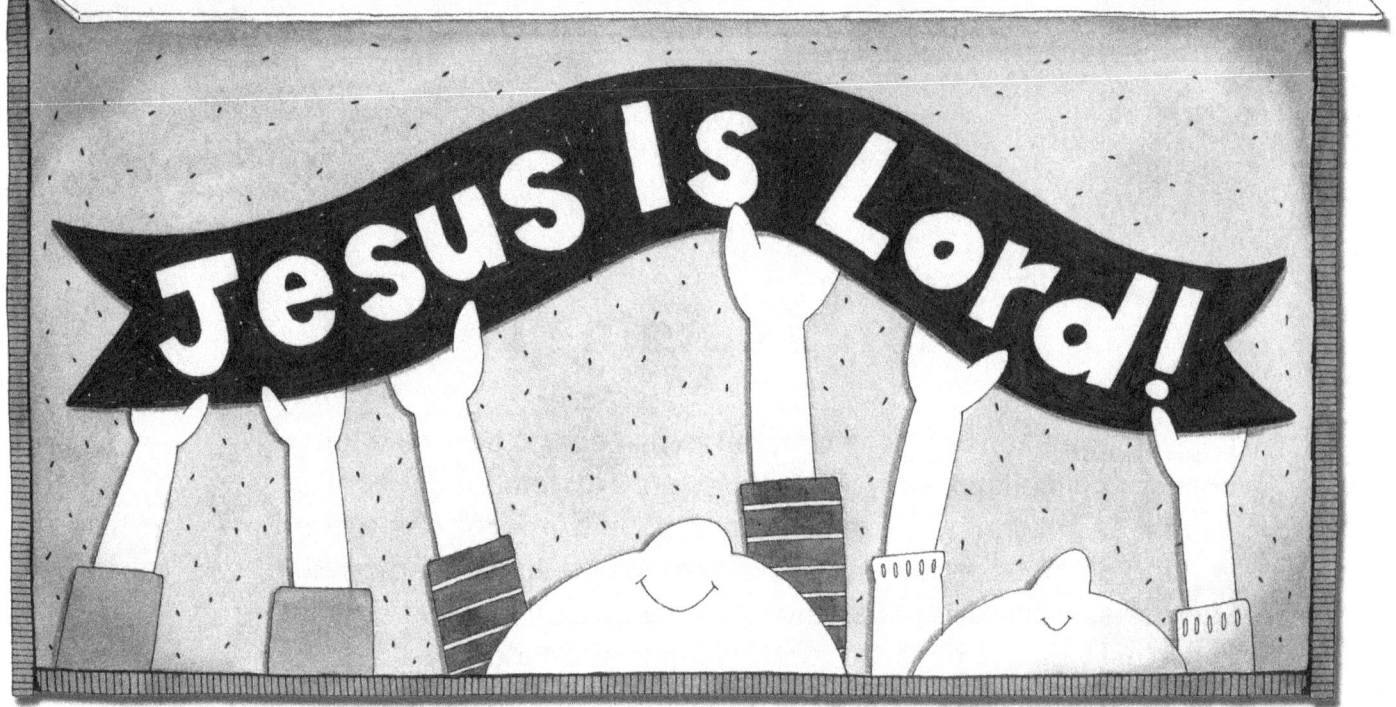

Jesus Is Lord!

SIMPLE SUPPLIES

➤ scissors
➤ tape or stapler
➤ confetti or fireworks-print gift wrap
➤ 3-inch-wide red ribbon
➤ construction paper
➤ various colors of ribbon
➤ face and arm patterns from pages 96 and 97
➤ markers

SIMPLE DIRECTIONS

1 Cover the bulletin board with confetti or fireworks-print gift wrap or blue background paper. Add a border made from wide red ribbon.

2 Construct and attach a shelf across the top of the display. Cut red, white, and blue construction paper letters to spell the title of the display. Attach each letter to a small ramp. Then tape the letters and ramps to the shelf.

3 Photocopy the face and arm patterns from pages 96 and 97 onto pink, brown, and yellow construction paper to represent ethnic diversity. Photocopy one face pattern and one set of arms onto each color of paper.

4 Pin, staple, or tape the faces to the bottom of the display, leaving enough space between each one for the matching arms. Cut ribbon or construction paper sleeves for the arms, then attach pairs of arms along the bottom of the display. Be sure they're pointing upward.

5 Cut a large, red construction paper banner as shown in the illustration. Add white construction paper letters to spell "Jesus Is Lord!" Affix the banner so that it looks as if the pairs of hands are holding the banner high in the air.

More Learning Fun!

➤ Make banners from 2-by-4-foot lengths of shelf paper or white cotton fabric. Provide permanent markers and fabric paints, and invite kids to embellish their own banners for Christ. Encourage kids to use Christian symbols, such as doves, crosses, fish, or hearts on their banners. Allow the banners to dry thoroughly before hanging them around the church for a colorful display of your allegiance.

➤ Read aloud Psalm 20:5; 60:4; and Song of Solomon 2:4. Talk about why we want to hold our banners for Jesus high so everyone can see them. Encourage kids to tell ways they can show they follow Jesus, such as being kind to others, donating clothes and toys to homeless shelters, or baking cookies for sick friends.

➤ Have kids trace and cut out their own hand prints from construction paper. Let kids sign their paper hands, then attach them to the display.

➤ Have fun with your kids making fun mini banner bookmarks. Cut 2-by-6-inch strips of colorful paper, and let kids embellish the bookmarks with markers, stickers, or glitter glue. Include one of the following verses on each bookmark: Psalm 20:5, Psalm 60:4, or Song of Solomon 2:4. Have kids present the bookmarks to the children in another class.

Bible Balloon Trivia

SIMPLE SUPPLIES

➤ scissors
➤ tape or stapler
➤ confetti-print gift wrap
➤ yellow and orange crepe paper
➤ red, yellow, and orange construction paper
➤ two bags of balloons
➤ pencils and small slips of paper
➤ various colors of curling ribbon

SIMPLE DIRECTIONS

1 Cover the bulletin board with confetti-print gift wrap. Add a border of twisted together. You may wish to add streamers of curled ribbon to the corners of your display.

2 Make a title board or cut out individual letters to spell the title, "BIBLE BALLOON TRIVIA." If you cut out letters, consider using balloons for the two "O's" in the word "balloon."

3 Let your kids take it from here! Hand each child two balloons, a pencil, and two small slips of paper. Let each child write a question pertaining to a particular lesson you're studying or a question from a previous lesson—for example, he or she might write "What was the name of David's best friend?" or "Which book of the Bible comes before the book of Revelation?"

4 Instruct kids to fold their slips of paper and push them inside their balloons. Then have kids blow up and tie off their balloons. Tie pieces of curled ribbon around the balloon knots, then tape the balloons to the bulletin board.

5 Form two groups and let groups take turns choosing balloons from the board. The groups must sit on the balloons to pop them, then read and answer the questions.

TERRIFIC TIP!

You may wish to repeat the game each week for a month as a great way to review material learned the week before. At the end of the month, simply remove the title, then use the same background paper for a new display!

More Learning Fun!

➤ Invite kids to make "trivia game show contestants" with extra balloons. Provide construction paper, ribbon, scissors, and tape, then let kids add facial features, clothes, and goofy hair to their balloon people. Encourage kids to use permanent markers to write one Bible trivia question on the backs of their balloon people.

Jesus Can **STOP** the Storm

SIMPLE SUPPLIES

➤ scissors
➤ tape or stapler
➤ black background paper
➤ wood-grained self-adhesive paper
➤ construction paper
➤ gold glitter glue
➤ poster board
➤ markers
➤ fabric (optional)
➤ tacky craft glue
➤ patterns from pages 86, 87, and 88

SIMPLE DIRECTIONS

1 Cover the bulletin board with black background paper. Cut a yellow construction paper border of zigzag lightning streaks to go around the top and three-quarters of the display's sides. Add gold glitter glue to the edges of the lightning bolts.

2 Cut dark blue construction paper waves to go across the bottom of the display, and attach them flush with the bulletin board. Cut another set of waves from light blue construction paper, and add pedestals to the waves. Make sure that the light blue waves are smaller than the dark blue waves so that both sets of waves will show. Attach the light blue waves on top of the dark blue waves.

3 Use poster board to make a simple boat shape about 2-foot lengthwise. Cover the shape using wood-grained, self-adhesive paper. Position the boat between the waves in the center of the display.

4 Photocopy, enlarge, and color the patterns of Jesus and the disciples on pages 86, 87, and 88, or use patterns from an old Bible story coloring book. Cut out the patterns and color them. Cover Jesus' robe with fabric if desired. Position the figure of Jesus in the bow of the boat and the disciples peeking over the side.

5 Make a title board to attach above the display. Use a black marker to write the words "Jesus," "Can," and "Storm." Cut the word "Stop" from red construction paper, and attach small pedestals to the letters to lift the word off the title board. Position and attach the title board above the display.

More Learning Fun!

➤ Let children make construction paper faces to place in the boat with the disciples. As they work, talk about times the children have felt afraid, and point out that Jesus is always ready to help them. Remind kids that Jesus is bigger than any storm or any problem—Jesus can do anything!

➤ Invite your children to act out the story of Jesus calming the stormy sea. Turn a table upside down for a boat, then choose someone to play the part of Jesus and a few children to play the parts of the frightened disciples. Have the rest of the children provide exciting storm sounds.

➤ If you're using this display with fourth- through sixth-grade children, let them use plastic knives to carve bars of Ivory soap into boats that really float! Younger children may wish to create a floating fleet from sponges.

➤ Set sail with your preschoolers and sing this fun, action song. Sing the song to the tune of "Row, Row, Row Your Boat."

Row, row, row your boat *(make rowing motions)*

With Jesus by your side— *(pat your side)*

You'll never have to be afraid *(shake your head "no")*

Of a splashy ride! *(make splashing motions)*

The Game Garden

SIMPLE SUPPLIES

➤ scissors
➤ tape or stapler
➤ cloud-print gift wrap
➤ brown burlap
➤ yellow and orange crepe paper
➤ neon paper
➤ construction paper
➤ poster board
➤ glitter glue in a variety of colors
➤ markers

SIMPLE DIRECTIONS

1 Cover the bulletin board with cloud-print gift wrap or blue background paper. Make a ground line using brown burlap. Add a border of lively yellow and orange crepe paper twisted together.

2 Cut yellow and orange construction paper letters to spell the title, "THE GAME GARDEN." Add small pedestals to the letters, then attach the title above the display.

3 Use brightly colored construction paper, neon papers, and poster board to make large flower heads. Be sure the flower heads are at least 8-inches wide and that the flowers stand at least 2-feet tall. (Use patterns from page 91 if desired.)

4 Use extra neon paper and glitter glue to embellish the flower heads and make them eye-popping! Use markers to add facial features to the flower heads. Mount the flower head cutouts on pedestals, with at least a foot of space between each flower.

5 Cut green construction paper stems and leaves, and attach them to the blossoms on the bulletin board. Add a few small, leafy "plants" between the flowers.

6 Position four pull-wires so that the loose ends dangle behind the flower heads, then tie paper clips on the ends. The paper clips will hold index cards for the game.

More Learning Fun!

➤ To use this display as a great class review game, simply write questions about a particular lesson or Bible story on index cards. and attach them to the paper clips behind each flower. Have kids form two groups and take turns pulling the action wires to reveal the cards hiding behind the flowers. Score one point for each correctly answered question. Once all the questions have been answered, add more cards and continue to play.

➤ Invite kids to make their own beautiful blossoms to add to the display. Provide tape, glue, tissue paper, construction paper, markers, chenille wires, ribbon, and cupcake liners, then let kids go "wildflower wild"! When the flowers are done, attach them around the edges of the bulletin board.

➤ Make yummy, edible flowers by letting each child spread frosting on two sugar cookies, then sandwiching a clean craft stick between the cookies. Add dabs of icing to the outsides of the cookies and stick dried fruits and small candies on as flower petals.

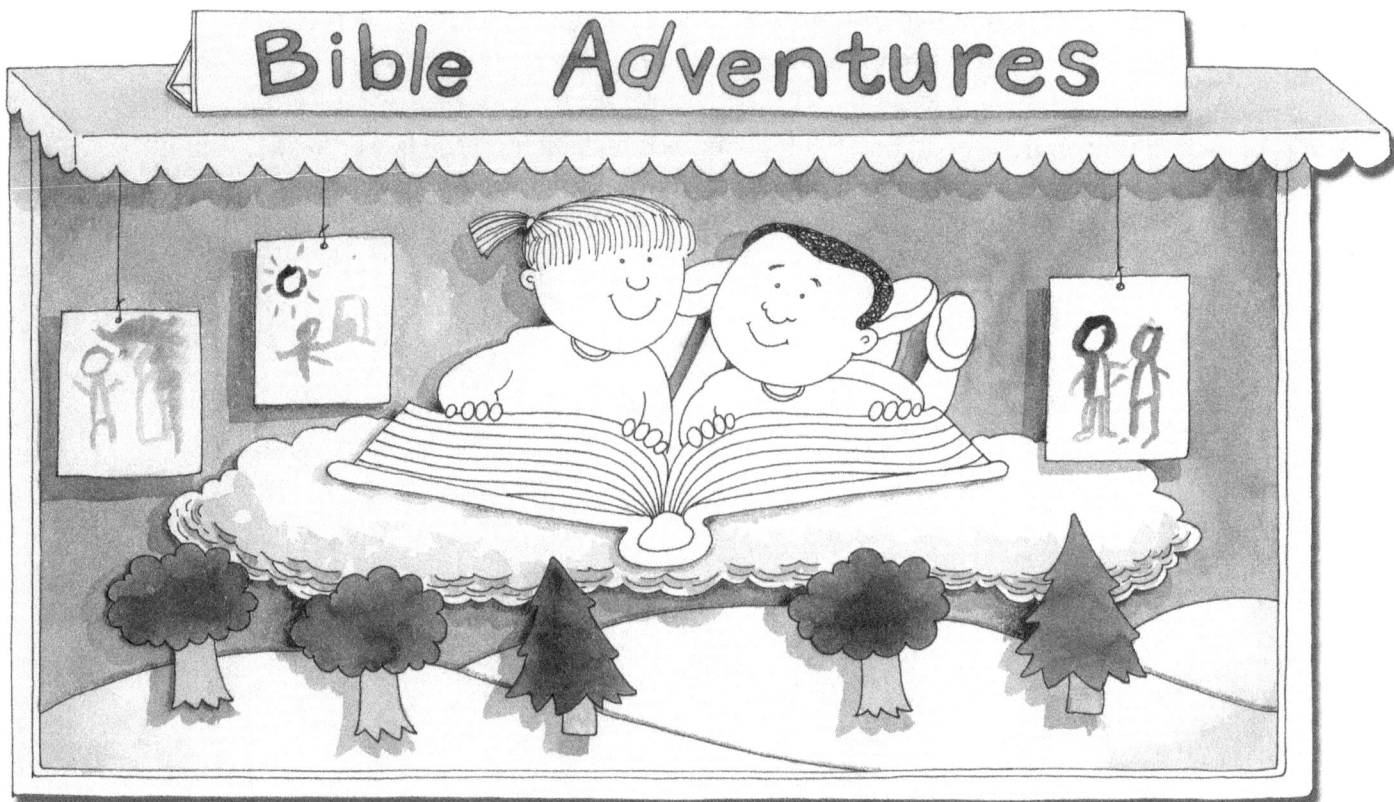

Bible Adventures

SIMPLE SUPPLIES

➤ scissors

➤ tape or a stapler

➤ light blue background paper

➤ green construction paper

➤ batting

➤ fishing line

➤ white paper

➤ markers and crayons

➤ photocopies of the children and Bible from page 84 and trees from page 91

SIMPLE DIRECTIONS

1 Cover the bulletin board with light blue background paper. (Cloud gift wrap would make a nice background as well!)

2 Cut green construction paper "hills" and attach them along the bottom third of the display. Add lines using markers to make the hills appear layered.

3 Make and attach a shelf to go across the top of your display. Create a title board that says "Bible Adventures" or "Flyin' High With God's Word!" Attach the title board to the shelf.

4 Photocopy, enlarge, and color the "children with a Bible" and tree patterns on pages 84 and 91. Cut out the patterns and color them using markers or crayons.

5 Mount the trees on pedestals at the bottom of the display.

6 Staple or tape batting clouds around the children with a Bible figure. Fasten the trees to the rolling hills. (Placing pedestals behind some of the trees will give them a nice 3-D look!)

7 Illustrate several stories from the Old and New Testaments on sheets of white copy paper. You may wish to have children do the illustrating! Then hang the drawings from the shelf or along the bottom of the display.

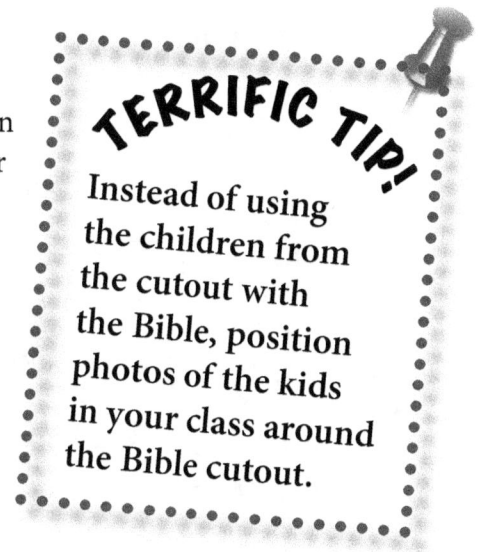

TERRIFIC TIP!

Instead of using the children from the cutout with the Bible, position photos of the kids in your class around the Bible cutout.

More Learning Fun!

➤ Write the books of the Bible on index cards, then let your kids tape them in order around the edges of the bulletin board.

➤ Add peek-a-boo flaps over the children's drawings. Uncover a new drawing each week, then read the Bible story that is depicted for great reviews or "sneak peeks."

➤ Sing a favorite song "The B-I-B-L-E." Let kids point to the letters in the word "Bible" on your display as you sing.

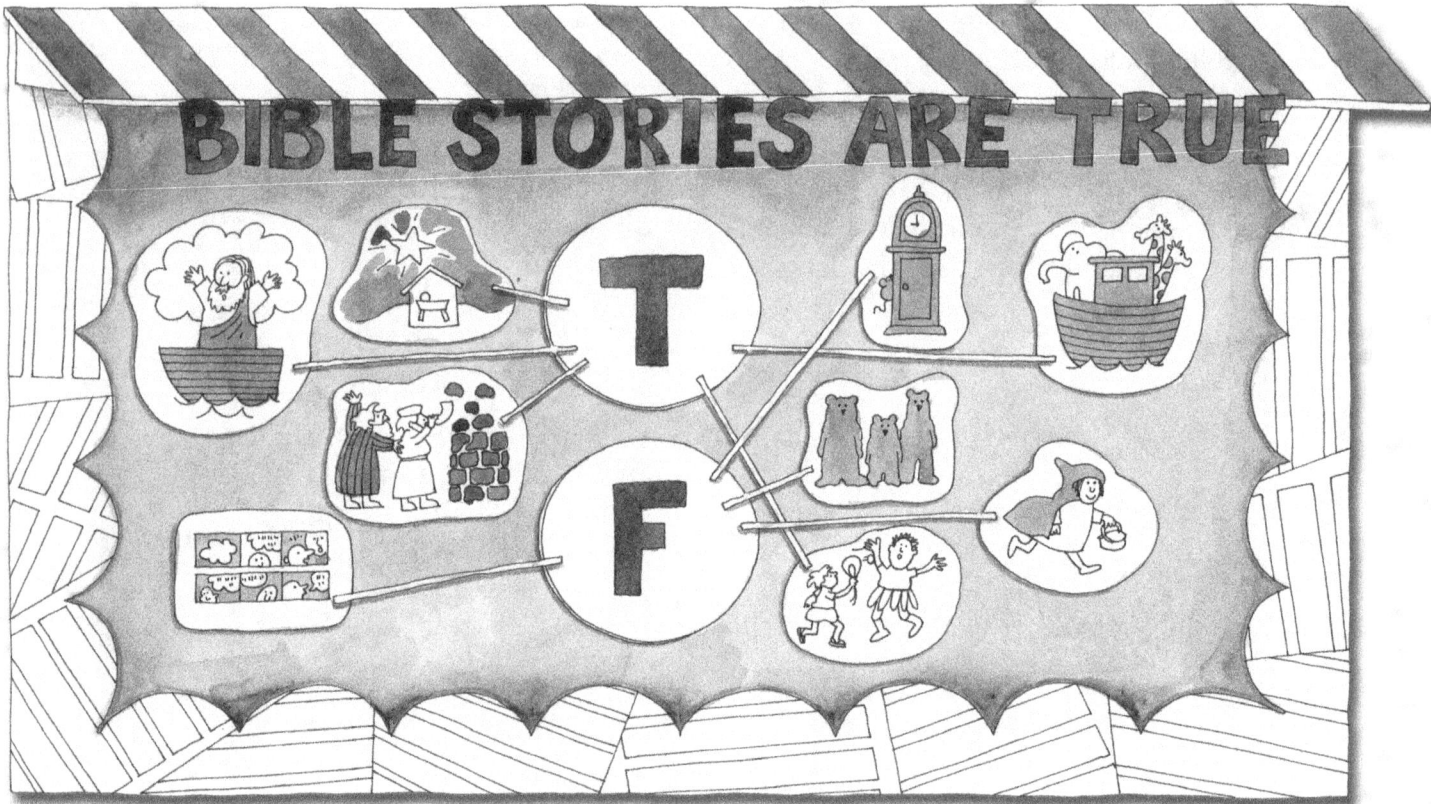

BIBLE STORIES ARE TRUE

SIMPLE SUPPLIES

➤ scissors

➤ tape or stapler

➤ blue background paper

➤ Sunday comics

➤ striped paper or fabric

➤ yellow and red construction paper

➤ 3 sheets of yellow poster board

➤ yarn

➤ push pins or tacks

➤ Bible coloring books

SIMPLE DIRECTIONS

1 Cover the bulletin board with blue background paper. Add a wide border using colorful Sunday newspaper comics.

2 Construct and attach an awning to span the top of the display. Cover the awning with brightly striped paper or fabric.

3 Cut yellow construction paper letters for the title, and hang them along the front edge of the awning.

4 Cut two 8-inch circles from yellow poster board. Attach them to the center of the display, one above the other. Tape a large red construction paper "T" (for the word "true") to the top circle and an "F" (for "false") to the circle on the bottom.

5 Check secular and Christian coloring books to find the following real and imaginary pictures (you may use the patterns at the back of this book as well). Color and cut out the pictures, and attach them to large poster board shapes such as squares, circles, hearts, stars, and triangles.

- **Real story picture suggestions:** Jesus' birth, Noah and the ark, David and Goliath, Jesus calming the storm, Joshua at the walls of Jericho.

- **Imaginary story picture suggestions:** The Three Bears, Little Red Riding Hood, pictures from the Sunday newspaper comics.

6 Attach the poster board shapes around the display, then cut lengths of yarn to reach from the pictures to the letters T or F. Pin five ends of yarn on the letter T and three ends on the letter F. Invite kids to pin the dangling ends of yarn to the appropriate pictures showing whether the picture is real (as in Bible stories) or imaginary (as in fairy tales or comics).

More Learning Fun!

➤ Let kids make their own comic strips. At an office supply store, purchase a sheet of transparency film for each child. Let kids use colorful permanent markers to draw and color cartoons. As kids work, remind them that all the stories in the Bible are true and that we can trust what the Bible tells us. When kids finish let them tape the comic strips on a window to let the light shine through.

➤ If you have older kids in class, let them make cartoon "flip books." Before class, use a paper cutter to cut 4-inch squares of paper. Cut at least 20 squares for each child and staple the squares into books of 20 pages each. Hand each child a blank book and invite him or her to draw successive pictures on each page. Suggest the walls of Jericho tumbling down or the Red Sea parting. When each page contains a picture, have kids flip through the pages to make the cartoons come alive with action.

➤ Compare and contrast fairy tales, nursery rhymes, and other children's stories with real stories from the Bible. Ask questions such as "Why do you think God would put only true stories in the Bible?" and "How can we trust what we read in the Bible?"

➤ Let children form pairs, and have each draw a picture that's either from a fairy tale or from the Bible. Then attach the pictures to the display and use yarn to match the pictures to the letters T or F.

SIMPLE DIRECTIONS

SIMPLE SUPPLIES

- scissors
- tape or stapler
- yellow or brown background paper
- newspapers
- construction paper
- craft items such as craft sticks, feathers, fabric, tissue paper, ribbon, sand paper, and aluminum foil
- patterns from page 89

1 Cover the bulletin board with brown or yellow background paper. Attach a border of crumpled newspaper "stones." (Your children will enjoy making this border and taping it in place!)

2 Cut out letters to spell: *"Goliath had a tiny heart—David had a GIANT heart!"* Attach the letters to the display as shown in the illustration. You may wish to cut out heart shapes to replace the word "heart."

3 Enlarge and photocopy the patterns for David and Goliath on page 89. (Be sure the picture of Goliath is much larger than the picture of David.) Cut out the figures.

4 Let children color and embellish the pictures, using a variety of sensory materials such as sandpaper, feathers, aluminum foil, and fabric.

5 Attach the figures of David and Goliath to the bulletin board. Tape a paper wad "stone" between the figures of David and Goliath.

TERRIFIC TIP!
You may wish to cut sponges in to stone-like shapes to attach to your display in place of paper wads. Young kids will enjoy sponge painting with the stones later!

More Learning Fun!

➤ Let children try their aim at bowling over Goliath. Photocopy the figure of Goliath and tape it to a paper cup. Hand each child a small ball made from a wad of masking tape. (Be sure the sticky side of the tape is facing out.) Take turns tossing the tape balls at the figure of Goliath. Each time a tape ball sticks to Goliath, have the class say, *"The battle is the Lord's!"* or *"God always wins!"*

➤ Invite children to use acrylic or tempera paints to paint heart shapes on smooth stones. When the paint is dry, spray the stones with hair spray, and have children use the stones as paperweights to remind them that God looks at our hearts when he sees us.

➤ Your young children will enjoy a game of opposites. Point out how David was small while Goliath was big and that David's heart was kind while Goliath's heart was mean. Say the following words, when kids know a word that means the opposite, have them put their fingers on their noses, then say the opposite word.

• happy (sad)	• tall (short)	• stop (go)
• down (up)	• fast (slow)	• inside (outside)

Don't Be a Turkey... Count Your Blessings!

SIMPLE SUPPLIES

➤ scissors
➤ tape or stapler
➤ yellow background paper
➤ a variety of men's neckties
➤ brown, yellow, red, and orange construction paper
➤ crepe paper
➤ pumpkin cutouts (optional)

SIMPLE DIRECTIONS

1 Cover the bulletin board with yellow background paper.

2 Use men's neckties stapled end-to-end around the edges of the display. Or twist lengths of yellow, orange, and brown crepe paper together and tape or staple them in place as a colorful border.

3 Draw a large turkey head, neck, and legs on brown construction paper or poster board. Add a yellow construction paper beak and a red paper comb and "gobbler." (See illustration)

4 Attach the turkey's head to a pedestal, then attach it to the bulletin board. Pin men's neckties around the base of the neck to create a body with unique tail feathers.

5 Cut large pumpkins from orange construction paper. Add 3-D pumpkin stems by rolling strips of brown construction paper and taping them in place on the pumpkins. Pin or staple the pumpkins around the turkey.

6 Add a shelf at the top of the display and attach a title board. Create a subtitle board that says, *"Count Your Blessings!"* and tape it to the edge of the shelf so that it hangs down.

TERRIFIC TIP!

Be crafty and let your kids make pumpkin prints by dipping carved pumpkin bits in tempera paint, then stamping the pumpkin shapes on paper plates. Add brown or green construction paper stems, then hang the artwork from the ceiling to create a suspended pumpkin patch!

More Learning Fun!

➤ Have kids write or draw a "thank you" on each of the pumpkins in the display. Invite church members to read and enjoy your class praises and thank-yous to God.

➤ Let younger kids practice their counting skills with Mr. Gobbler. Write numbers from 1 to 10 on index cards, then challenge kids to pin number cards in sequence on the pumpkins to discover how many pumpkins are in the patch.

➤ Make "praise pudding" by adding a few tablespoons of canned pumpkin to prepared vanilla pudding and stirring well. As you enjoy your treat, encourage kids to share ways they can thank God this week such as praying, being kind to others, or helping at home.

The Brightest Star by Far

SIMPLE SUPPLIES

- scissors
- tape or stapler
- black or dark blue background paper
- gold and silver glitter glue
- yellow poster board
- brown paper grocery sack
- fishing line or string
- eyelet screws
- paper clips
- patterns from pages 80, 81, and 82

SIMPLE DIRECTIONS

1 Cover the bulletin board with black or dark blue background paper or star-print gift wrap with a dark background. Cut a construction paper border using the star pattern on page 14 (or use sparkly Christmas garland).

2 Cut title letters from yellow construction paper and tape them across the top of the display.

3 Cut two large, dark blue construction paper clouds and attach them with pedestals to the display. You'll want space in back of the clouds for figures to "hide" behind. Add a yellow poster board star to the center top of the display. Embellish the star using glitter glue.

4 Cut a green construction paper bush and a hill shape and attach them to the bulletin board using pedestals. Then cut and form a stable from a brown paper grocery sack and attach the stable to the bulletin board using a pedestal. All of these figures must have spaces behind them for the pull-wires to work correctly.

5 Photocopy, enlarge, and color the figures on pages 80, 81, and 82. You may wish to copy the figures using stiff card stock paper. Cut out the patterns and set them aside until the pull-wires are in place.

6 Set up a series of four pull-wires (using fishing line or string) according to the illustration. Tape the figures to the ends of the appropriate wires so that when they're not being pulled, they're "hiding" behind the correct display elements—for example, the angels are hiding behind the clouds and the wise men are hiding behind the hill.

TERRIFIC TIP!

For an appealing ceiling with sparkle and pizzazz, cover the ceiling area, or a portion of the ceiling, with black plastic garbage bags. Suspend glittery stars from the ceiling. You may even wish to have the door activate pull-wires that will make the stars to go up and down each time the door is opened or closed!

More Learning Fun!

➤ Cut poster board star patterns of varying sizes. Provide aluminum foil and show kids how to tear off pieces of foil, then wrap the foil around the stars, molding it to the stars' shapes. Tape a length of fishing line to each star, then suspend the stars from coat hangers for shiny mobiles.

➤ Make delicious star snacks to enjoy. Use star-shaped cookie cutters to cut stars from fresh bread. Let kids spread butter on top of the star shapes, then sprinkle colored, decorative sugar over the butter for shiny, sparkly treats.

➤ Preschoolers and young children will enjoy the following game. Sing "Little Shepherd, Where Are You?" to the tune of "Mary Had a Little Lamb." Assign the roles of shepherd, angel, sheep, or wise men to pairs of children. As you sing the song, fill in the name of one of the roles. Let children with that role go to the display and pull the appropriate pull-wire. Sing and play until everyone has had a turn to pull an action wire on the bulletin board.

Little *(name of role)*, **where are you?**
Where are you? Where are you?
Little *(name of role)*, **where are you?**
Jesus Christ is born!

PATTERNS

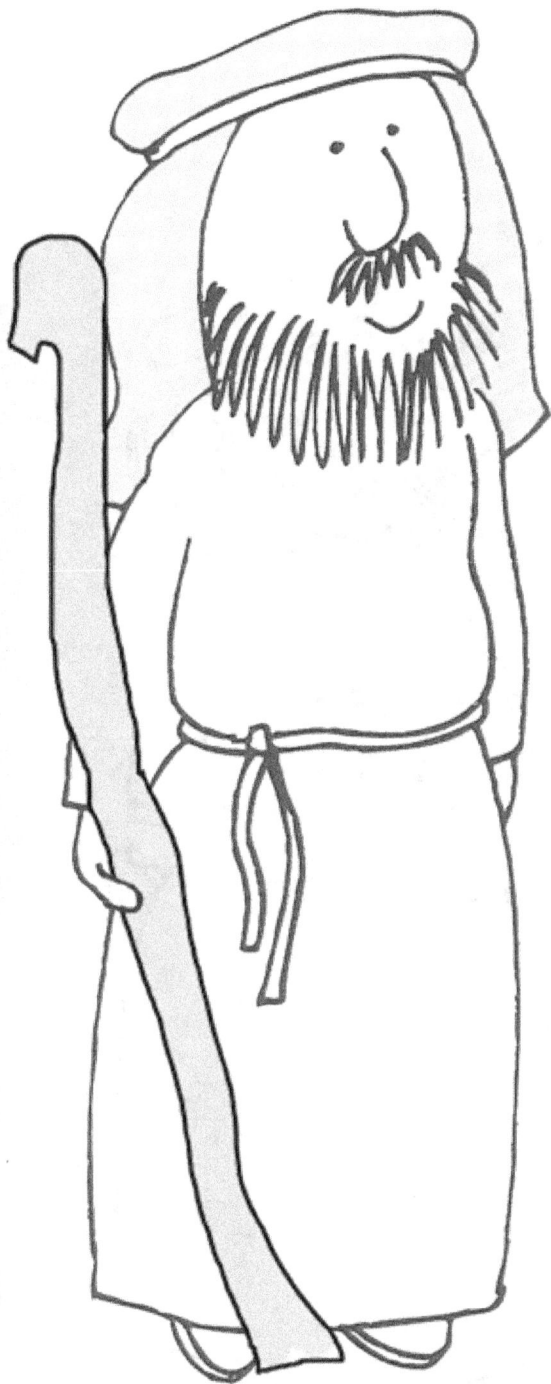

81

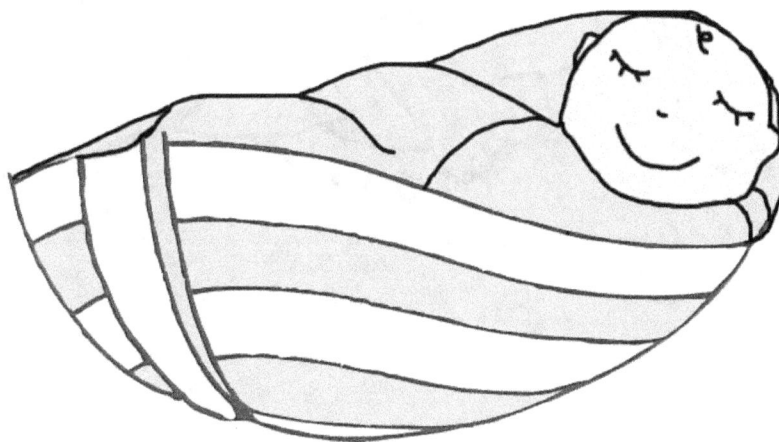

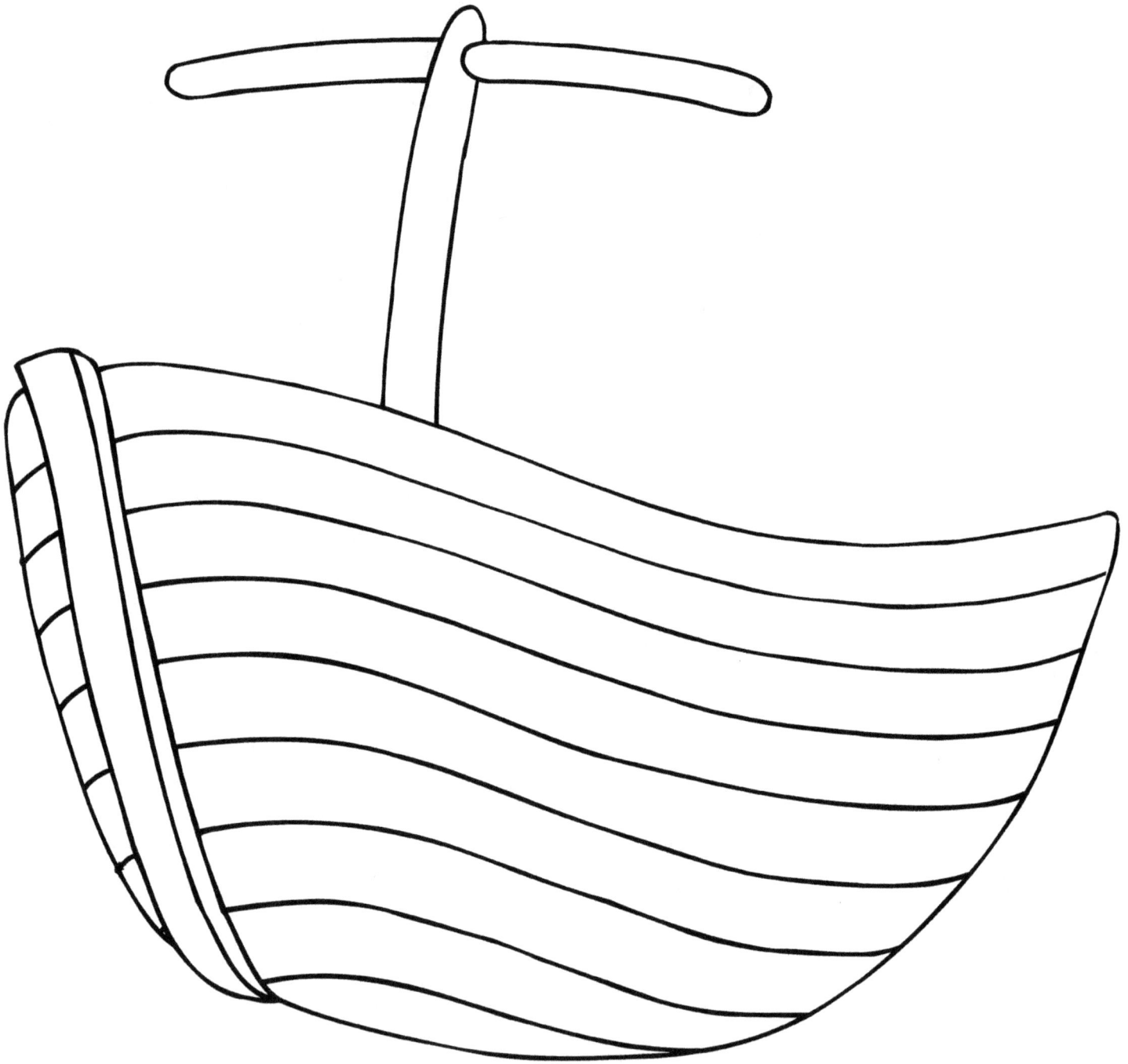

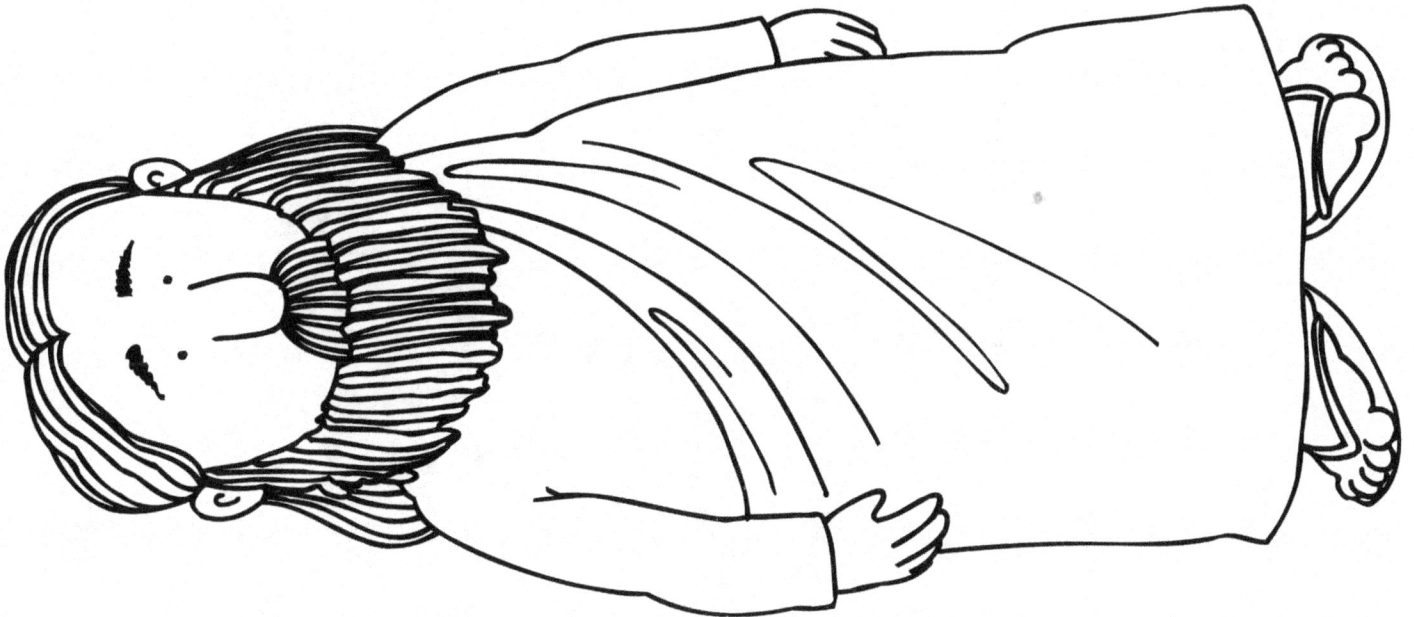

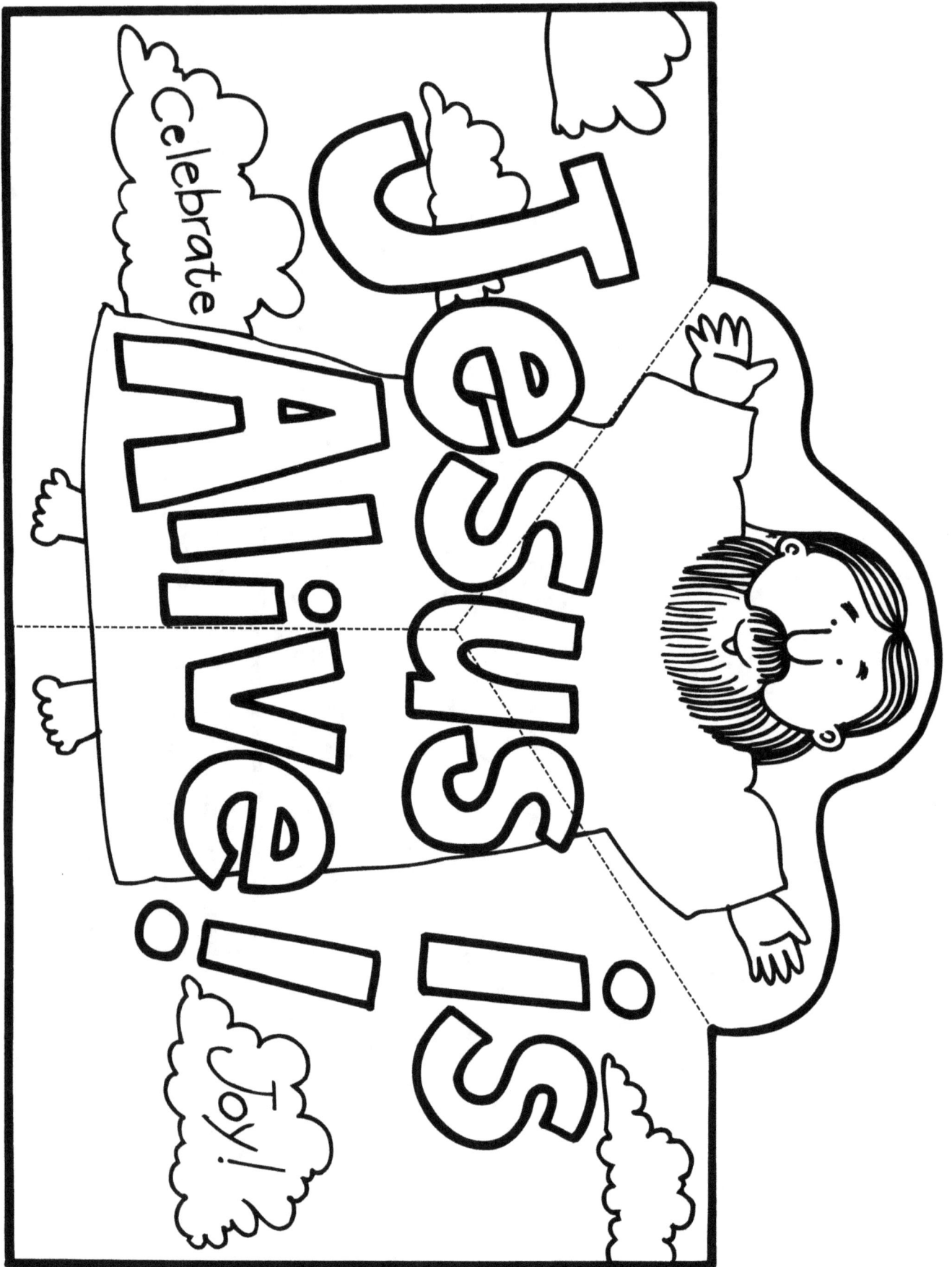

Celebrate

Jesus is Alive!

Joy!

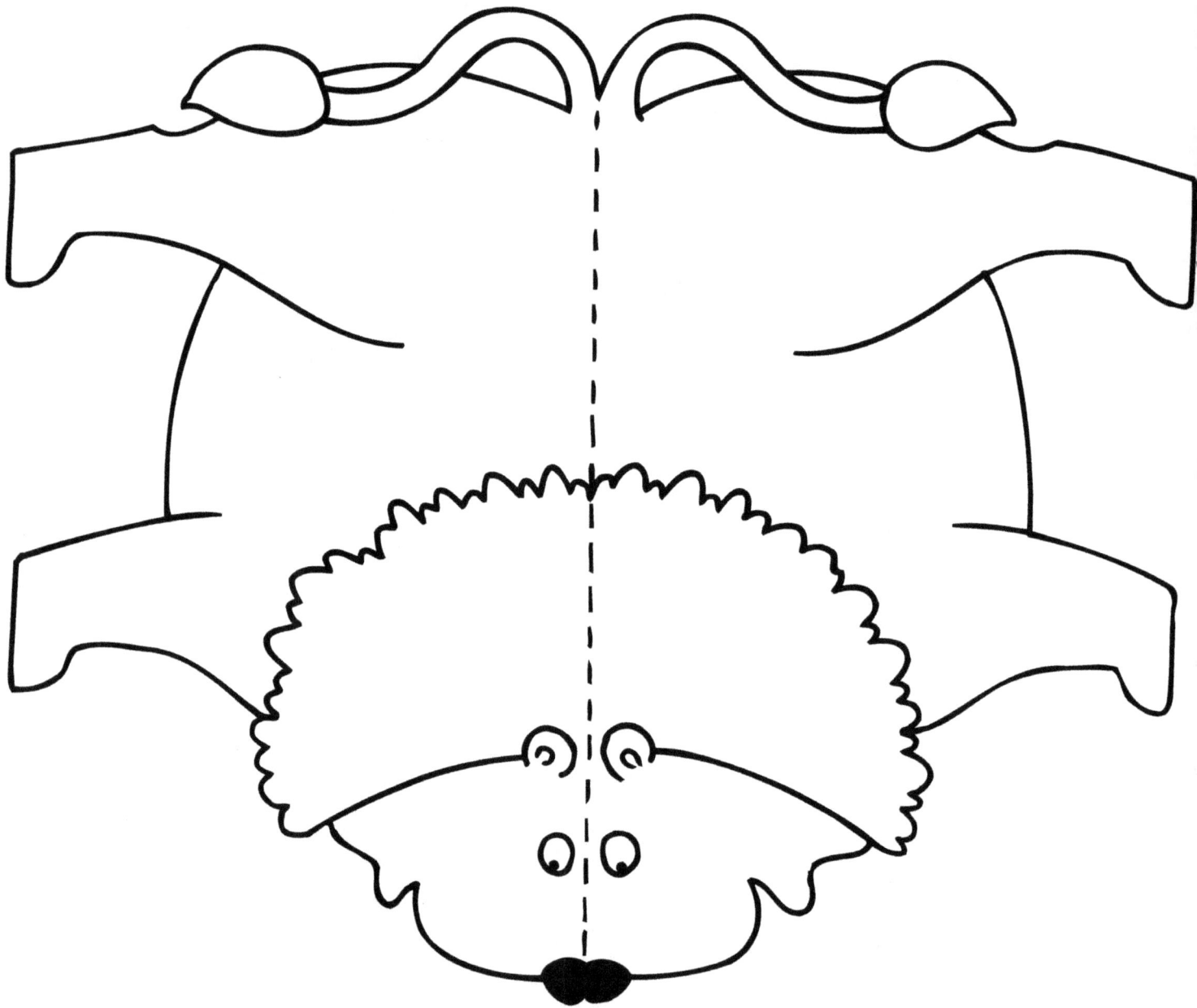

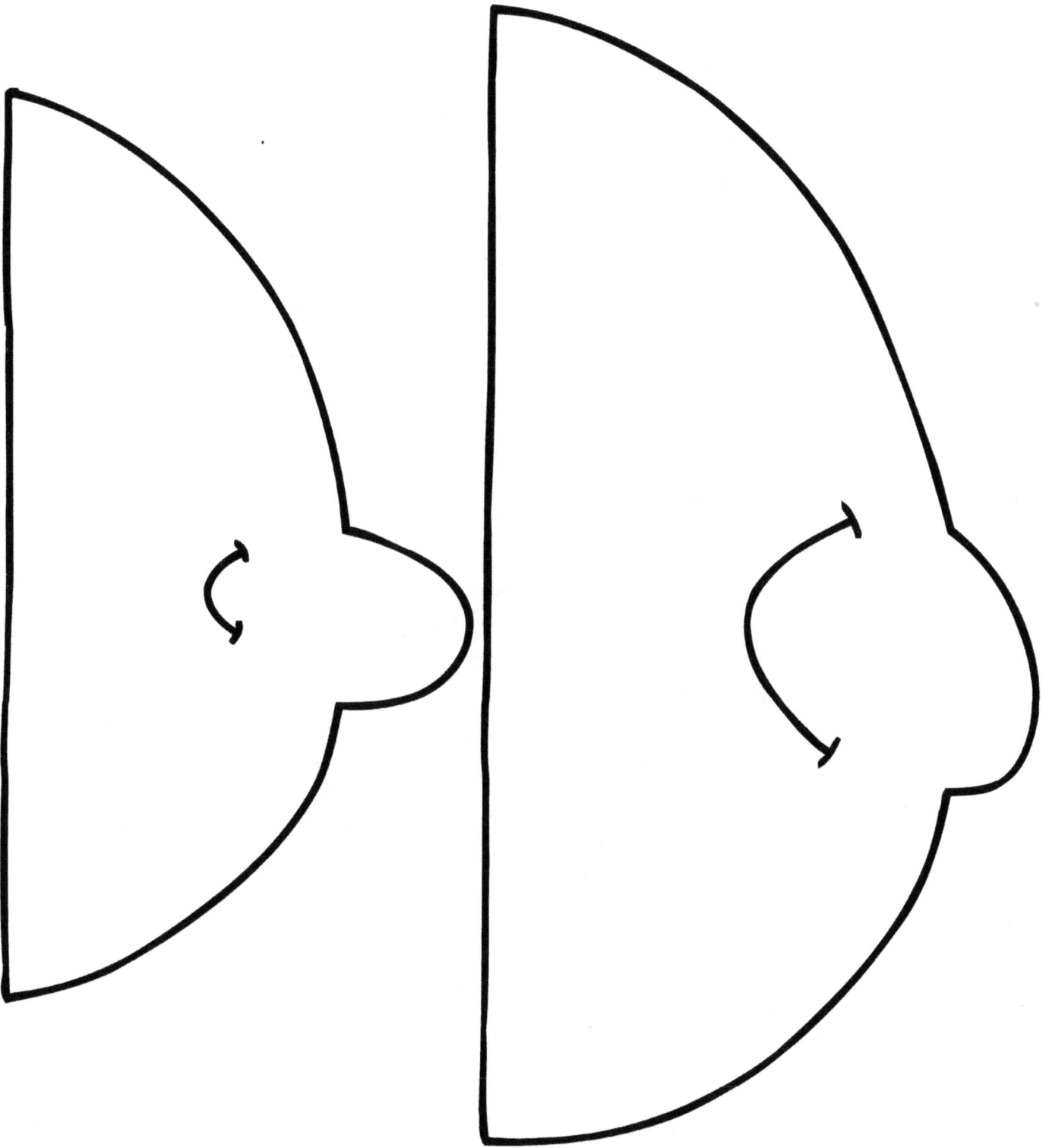

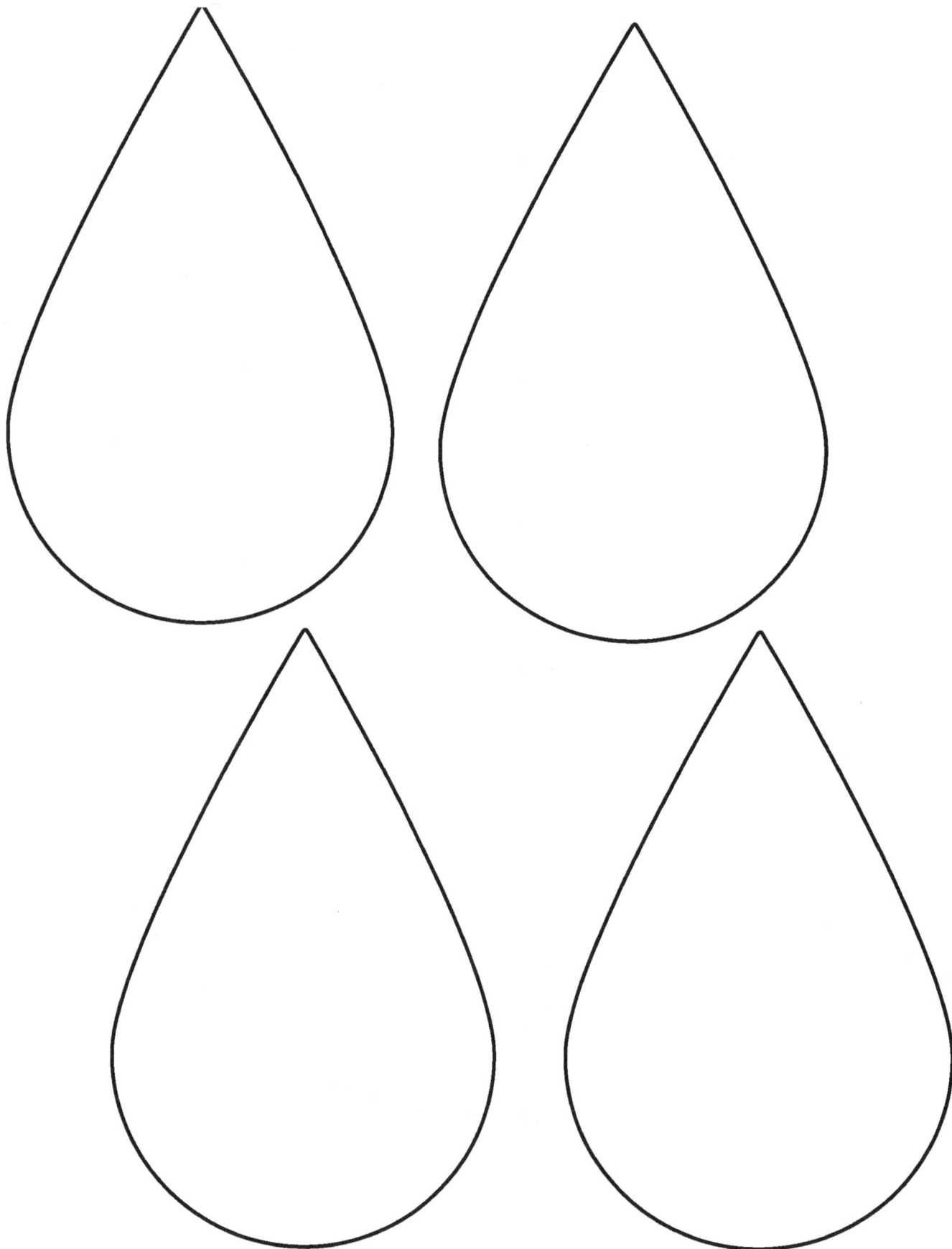

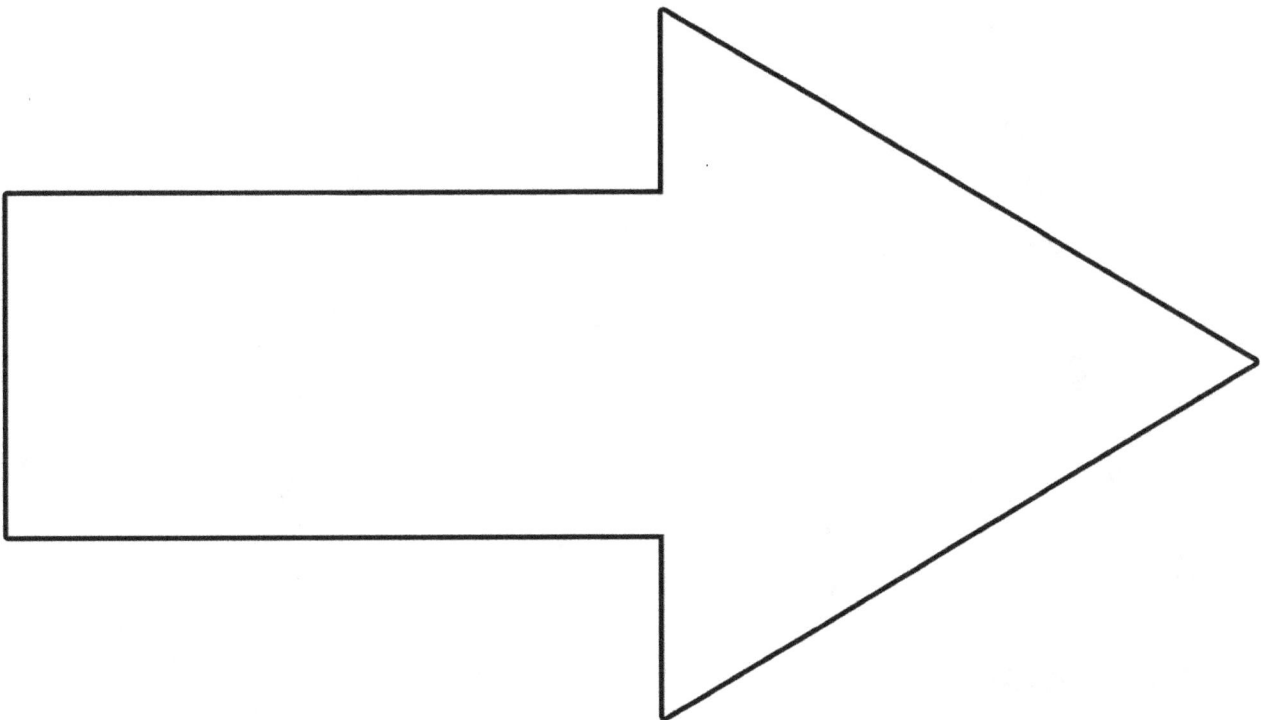